THE PERSONAL LEADERSHIP PUZZLE

ALSO BY SUSAN K. WEHRLEY

Books

The Secret to "I AM": A True Story...
Discover Courage, Truth,
Purpose and Peace in Difficult Times

The Secret to "I AM": Discover Your Story...
Discover Your Purpose

The Secret to "I AM": Wisdom Tips and Workbook

The Power to Believe:
Overcoming Fear and Self-Doubt
to Create the Life you Want!

The Power to Believe:
I AM Creating the Life I Want–Journal/Workbook

Audio Programs

The Secret to "I AM" Wisdom Tips

The Secret to "I AM": A True Story...
Discover Courage, Truth,
Purpose and Peace in Difficult Times

Videotapes

The Secret to "I AM" Sensory Seminar

THE PERSONAL LEADERSHIP PUZZLE

8 MISSING PIECES TO A COMPLETE LIFE!

By Susan K. Wehrley

Thomas & Kay

Publishers of books that make a difference!

Publisher:
Thomas & Kay, LLC

For further information on other
Susan K. Wehrley Books, Programs, and Services
contact: (262) 691-5001 or www.solutionsbysusan.com

Editing by Nancy Peske
Illustrations by Karen M. Wiltz
Book Interior by Vilar Arts
Susan K. Wehrley photo by A.K. Photography

FIRST EDITION

ISBN

10 9 8 7 6 5 4 3 2 1

FOR MY BROTHER

Thank you for teaching me to live life to the fullest
and how to create a legacy.

My brother, Gary J. Morrison, was born to eternal life,
Thursday, September 21, 2006, the day after I finished this book.

CONTENTS

INTRODUCTION

In my 20 years as a business and personal coach and trainer, thousands of people have come to me for the same reason: They are trying to figure out the missing pieces that will complete their life.

That is why I have developed *The Personal Leadership Puzzle: 8 Missing Pieces to a Complete Life!* Personal leadership is a commitment to live a conscious and connected life by noticing eight missing pieces that fit together and create in us a sense of fulfillment and effectiveness.

In some cases, people feel they have a life filled with abundance, but they have lost the clarity of its purpose and the day-to-day love they once felt for the people they were in relationship with, their jobs, and their activities. They have the house, the job, the health, the spouse, the kids, etc., but feel they have no zest left for life. In other cases, people mistakenly believe that if they could just get what they think are the missing pieces in their life-the right house, the really fabulous job, better health, the perfect spouse, or a child-then they'd feel complete. Whatever the case is, most people are looking for that missing piece that they feel is keeping them from feeling fulfilled and effective. They may think there's "a" missing piece but actually there are eight. If they were conscious of these missing pieces, they would feel more empowered.

My clients aren't the only ones struggling to feel a sense of fulfillment and contentment. People today are dealing with more divorce, debt, addictions, anxiety, and depression disorders than ever before. The United States Commission on Mental Health concluded that one person in seven living in the U.S. will at some time or another require professional treatment for an emotional disturbance. From 1991 to 1999 alone, the use of antidepressants more than doubled. Currently, 18.8 million

American adults, or 9.5 percent of the U.S. population 18 years or older, are suffering from depression, with women affected twice as often as men. The effects of depression and anxiety have cost businesses $24 billion in lost work each year. In addition, one in five children have been diagnosed with a mental, emotional, or behavioral disorder (Surgeon General's Report on Mental Health, 1999).

Instead of turning inward to become aware of these eight missing pieces that are causing us anxiety and depression, we have become a society dependent on medication to recenter us. In some cases, of course, it is necessary to take such medication, especially when the emotional disturbance is due to a chemical imbalance in the brain. However, with or without medication, we can all benefit by learning to lead our lives in a more conscious way, using skills that will enable us to feel complete.

I wrote about the eight missing pieces to a complete life so that you can ask yourself some hard questions in order to determine whether you have all of the eight pieces integrated into your daily living, at work and at home. Fitting together the pieces of the personal leadership puzzle requires work, but the effects are very powerful. Being aware of the eight missing pieces and drawing upon them as needed will allow you to build and sustain the life you want.

My ideas about the process of gathering the eight missing pieces were developed as I taught clients how they could find inner fulfillment and feel a sense of effectiveness as they moved forward toward reaching their goals, at work and at home. This book is full of real stories from my coaching experiences (of course, the names and some minor details have been changed to protect the identity of the individuals). It also offers advice on developing the skills you need in order to obtain the eight missing pieces, skills that the people who have attended my training and coaching programs have found extremely useful.

........Although most people would say that they want their

dreams to come true, I have witnessed throughout the years that many people fear success or failure, and their fear holds them back from feeling complete. They may believe that success automatically brings stress and the need to sacrifice things that are important to them. They may fear failure, believing that if they open their heart and feel the full force of their passion and desire, and have faith that they can achieve their goals, but then they never quite get to where they thought they should be, they will feel devastated.

If you are without the eight pieces I describe in this book, you may feel anxious, defeated, unfulfilled, and ineffective in creating the life you want for yourself. Or, you might feel you have the right relationships, right job, right house, and right state of health, and yet you see your life as incomplete. If so, these eight pieces have gotten lost in the shuffle of your life somehow.

When you become aware of the eight missing pieces and bring them together, you can build and sustain a complete life. I want to help you identify the root cause of why you feel that your life is not fulfilling and that you are not empowered, and show you how you might live differently by practicing personal leadership every day.

Susan

Susan K. Wehrley

THE PERSONAL LEADERSHIP PUZZLE

"Be very careful, then, how you live –

not as unwise but as wise,

making the most of every opportunity..."

(Ephesians 5:15-16)

8 MISSING PIECES TO A COMPLETE LIFE!

First Piece: Get Curious! Live in the Wonder of Life

Second Piece: Get Clear! Slow Down to See Beyond the Fog

Third Piece: Get Calm! Find the Peace in the Storm

Fourth Piece: Get Confident! Fly Free from Worry

Fifth Piece: Get Caring! Open Your Heart to Love

Sixth Piece: Get Committed! Overcome Obstacles

Seventh Piece: Get Communicating! Call the Bird Out of the Bush

Eighth Piece: Get Creative! Discover the Field of Unlimited Possibilities

The first piece of the personal leadership puzzle is to get ***curious***. Curiosity is natural for children but somewhere along the way, most of us lost our sense of curiosity. When faced with difficulties, we don't see possibilities, we see only fog, and we feel lost. Instead of staying awake and alert to opportunities and ideas, we have become a society that has fallen asleep.

Curiosity leads us to becoming ***clear***, the second piece necessary for creating a life that feels complete. Getting clear is crucial because without an inner compass, we will be lost in the storm of life's distractions and pressures and start our day unfulfilled, powerless, and ineffective.

Becoming clear takes us to a higher level of self-awareness and awareness of life around us. This can cause us to feel anxious because, as we see the truth, we can begin to wonder if we are "enough" or have "enough"-enough power, enough intelligence, enough love, enough will, and so on-to overcome the obstacles we perceive. We need to learn to become ***calm*** amidst the storm, which is the third missing piece. Being calm allows us to move through life with more ease and less stress. As a result, we are able to feel more joy.

When we are calm, we can find the fourth piece, our more ***confident self***. This is the part of us that feels empowered even in the most difficult times and keeps us going no matter what the challenge.

When we've obtained the first four pieces to the personal leadership puzzle, we are able to take the action steps necessary to build a complete life. Often, however, we get as far as building a complete life but can't figure out how to sustain it. The remaining four pieces of the personal leadership puzzle allow us to do just that.

The fifth piece, get ***caring***, reminds us to be caring toward ourselves and not abandon our heart's desires as we remain caring toward others who are having difficulties with their own lives. Living according to the wisdom of a caring and compassionate heart allows us to love others as we love ourselves in spite of our human flaws and frailties.

It is from this loving connection that we can go forth and obtain the sixth piece to the personal leadership puzzle and become ***committed*** to our life's path. We're able to do this because we are energized by our own thoughts and feelings of love.

The seventh piece offers us a chance to become more aware of how our ***communication*** with ourselves and with others affects us along the way. As we increase our awareness of our internal and external communication, we quickly address issues and resolve them harmoniously, so that we can sustain a complete life rather than allowing adversity to distract us and drain us of energy.

Being able to love ourselves as we love others, through gathering the missing pieces of being caring, being committed, and having open communication, we can then obtain the final missing piece that helps us commune with our divine core, ultimately sustaining us. It is here at our core that we find our ***creativity***, which helps us to make decisions that are for the highest good of the all, thus creating mutually beneficial and loving partnerships in many areas of our lives-work, family, community, and so on.

FINDING THE PIECES

The Personal Leadership Puzzle offers you a new way to lead your life and your organization. It will teach you how to look honestly at yourself and take responsibility for choosing the missing piece you need in any given moment. It will show you how to catch yourself when you perceive yourself as a victim of circumstance just because things didn't turn out as you'd hoped or planned, or according to your timetable.

Although *The Personal Leadership Puzzle* can be read by itself, it's also designed to be a continuation of the themes in my first two books, *The Secret to "I AM"* and *The Power to Believe*, which were written to help people get rid of old, self-sabotaging patterns and empower them to create the life they want. It is my hope that *The Personal Leadership Puzzle* will help you to live out your life's dream in a less stressful and more satisfying way, by recognizing the missing pieces and making the conscious decision to obtain them and incorporate them into your life.

When writing this book, I realized that people are at different stages of development and therefore have different capacities to take in information. That is why I have written chapters with smaller sections within them so that, if necessary, you could read just one section or one piece to the personal leadership puzzle at a time, choosing to read the text that applies to your current situation. You may want to read a section or two and put the book down for a while, giving yourself time to fully absorb the information at hand.

Whether you choose to read the book one piece at a time, or read the various pieces as you need them, or start with reading the smaller sections that speak to your immediate needs, my hope for you is that you integrate these pieces in your life on a daily basis so that you can understand the full impact of personal leadership, at work and at home.

FIRST PIECE:

GET CURIOUS! LIVE IN THE WONDER OF LIFE

As we commit to a life of personal leadership, we humbly open ourselves up to discovering the missing pieces in our life and take responsibility for ourselves and our decisions. When we do this, we are able to live a more complete life and we become better equipped to positively affect the lives of the people around us, at work and at home. We realize that the best way to begin our journey of personal leadership is to discover the first of the 8 missing pieces needed to lead a complete life, which is to get curious and live in the wonder of life.

Getting curious means letting go of the static condition of our minds and the preconceived notions we hold regarding the world around us, others, and ourselves, so that we can be open to learn more. It is coupled with an openness to being in the unknown for a while until we are able to obtain the awareness and information we desire.

Getting curious requires us to have humility. We have to believe that we do not know it all if we're to be open to discovering that which is still foreign to us. Living with a curious mind allows us to realize that the more we know, the more we have to learn. When we live with a curious mind, we no longer feel shame about not knowing certain things or understanding them only with hindsight. We realize that even though we have reached a particular level of wisdom, we will continue to discover truth and learn more through our life experiences. We can become curious and learn from our new experiences, and instead of feeling shame that we discovered something we didn't know, we can say to ourselves, "Of course, I didn't know. I am always curious and learning!"

FREEING OURSELVES FROM THE OBSTRUCTIONS OF OUR MIND AND OUR WORLD OF BUSY-NESS HELPS US TO CHOOSE A LIFE OF CURIOSITY AND WONDER.

Overwhelmed . . . unfulfilled . . . powerless . . . anxious. These are feelings many people experience as they try desperately to create the life they want and then work hard to sustain it. Many people choose busy-ness over fulfillment and effectiveness, just so they don't have to experience how unfulfilled, powerless, and anxious they feel. Instead of going deeper to become more curious about the dilemma they are in, they just keep getting busier, missing the opportunity to slow down and find out who they are and what it is they need to have a complete life.

Whether it is your romantic relationship (or lack of), your employees, your boss, your kids, your finances, your weight, your commitments, or something else that is making you feel powerless and unhappy, it's important to ask yourself:

"How might I lead a more fulfilled and effective life?"

At work and in our personal lives, we often believe that the issues lie outside of ourselves. *We think, If only "they" would change-be more motivated, more committed, more open, more honest, more respectful* (and so on)-*I could be more happy and effective. If only this child or that boss would change, I could be satisfied and have a better life. If only my significant other would behave the way I want him to-or, if only I had a significant other-I could feel fulfilled.*

And when it comes to things like our weight and our finances, we often feel like a victim of circumstances. *If it weren't for all of those restaurants I have to eat out at and all the pressure I feel from society to spend more money, I wouldn't be in this situation.* We blame someone or something else, or the situation we are in, instead of being curious about the options before us.

If we are not shifting responsibility for our happiness to someone else, we're telling ourselves that we lack fulfillment and effectiveness because we don't have enough time or opportunities, or because we were dealt the wrong hand. When we are blaming someone or something else, we are avoiding the first piece of the personal leadership puzzle, which is to *get curious!*

At work or at home, it is always easier to blame our lack of fulfillment and our ineffectiveness on another person or a situation rather than becoming curious and discovering the root cause of our feelings, and our root need to transform our lives and bring about the changes we envision. We are afraid to become curious, because curiosity leads us into the unknown and that can make us feel unsettled, since we don't know what we might discover. Although at one level we love the feeling of openness and adventure, at another level, that kind of openness leaves us feeling emotionally vulnerable because we don't know what we may discover. Our ego, the part of us that likes to be right and in control, would rather quickly conjure up a conclusion and create a story in a given situation instead of being open and curious so we can grow.

Maybe if we get over the idea that there is someone to blame, or that someone is a "bad guy" who is responsible for our unhappiness, then we won't be so afraid that, *Uh oh, I might be the cause of this feeling and this outcome in my life (or at least in part)!* Changing our mindset from casting blame to learning our lessons in life can help us to realize that the truth will always set us free-free to make different choices in the future

WHEN YOU INCORPORATE PLAY IN YOUR EVERYDAY LIFE, YOU WILL BECOME MORE CURIOUS.

The technological boom has allowed us to move faster, get more information more quickly, connect with others more easily, and schedule ourselves more tightly. Although it is a blessing to be able to stay connected and to get more done, we often make these choices at the sacrifice of our own sanity.

We remain sane when we are able to stay connected to our curious-essence. That is difficult to do, however, when we are continually running around at high speed, going to meetings, answering cell phones, and checking our Blackberries for e-mails, all in one breath. Most of us have such jam packed days that even when the work day is done, we are still racing to our child's soccer game, to our health club, or to the salon to get our nails done. Heaven forbid we miss one of those commitments-we will be struck by guilt, feeling that we are not "enough": competent enough, parent enough, or man or woman enough.

In all our busy-ness, we often overlook the importance of play and forget we don't have to separate play from work or responsibilities. Play simply means being light-hearted. We can experience a playful spirit while cutting the lawn, having a meeting, or balancing our checkbook. If we go about life, at work and at home, with a playful spirit, we will stay connected to ourselves and our curious-essence and be mindful of our day.

Several people and situations come to mind when I think of being playful in the midst of responsibility. I recall:

- The client who sent me a funny cartoon by e-mail when I was expecting that I would be opening the last draft of a strategic plan. Opening up the document left me laughing at this surprise.

- The Christmas party we had when my daughter and I decided to break into a spontaneous dance routine we made up on the spot to "Frosty the Snowman," the song a spontaneous group of friends sang as they put together a playful band in the corner of the rec room.

- The song my daughter's boyfriend made up on the spot and sang to me one night when I came home and shared how a date went. He took the elements of what I told him, put it in poetic form, played the guitar with a familiar tune, and sang the highlights of my date back to me.

- The way my lawn maintenance man and I were joking and laughing about a fountain we were trying to put together in my yard. The directions did not match up with the parts in the box. We were joking and laughing about how the company needed the Susan K. Wehrley & Associates, Inc., cross-functional communication course, so that the person writing the instructions would actually look at the parts they were writing about! Instead of getting angry about it, we remained playful and laughed at the idea of contacting them for business.

- The time I broke into a cartwheel on the golf course because I hit my longest drive ever, or the time I did a cartwheel when my client climbed to the top of the wall when we were doing a Challenge Course.

To remain playful, we must commit to curiosity. Curiosity and having a sense of wonder bring playfulness to our daily chores and routines. Curiosity causes us to let go of fear: the fear of looking foolish. When we ask ourselves to entertain curious and "silly" thoughts that start with, "What if . . . ?" or "Wouldn't it be funny if . . . ?" or "I feel like (blank), why not?" or "I wonder how great it would feel if I just let go of my inhibitions?", we find the childlike curious-essence once again.

I remember working with a group of company vice presidents who were serious minded about doing strategic planning. I could see that the curious and creative juices were just not flowing and that they needed to be to open up to possibilities that would take the company where it needed to go to meet the aggressive goals they had in mind. To open them up to their curious-essence, I had each one of them bring to the next meeting a symbol of something that would tell the group something about themselves. We all laughed hard as people wore silly hats they got as souvenirs on vacation and brought playful stories to go along with them. The objects they brought and the stories they told helped them to go back into their playful state of minds once again. From that emotional place, we could find their curious-essence and begin our task with a fresh approach.

When we're living only to meet our daily responsibilities and check off the items on our list of "shoulds," without being curious and playful, we get caught up in a cycle of live to work, work to live, live to die. Now how boring and mundane is that?

Experience the innocence and wonderment of a little child: Incorporate play into your everyday life.

WE USE JUDGMENT AS A DEFENSE MECHANISM TO COVER OUR FEAR RATHER THAN GETTING CURIOUS ABOUT OURSELVES AND OTHERS, AND THE WONDROUS LIFE AROUND US.

It's easy to lose touch with our inner world and our priorities, and instead become focused on achieving our outer goals. When we do this, we can end up making quick judgments because we fear failure, and we can miss opportunities that present themselves-opportunities we would see if we allowed ourselves to become curious instead of fearful.

Being open to the wonder of life around us means we stay curious to the possibilities that don't come to mind quickly. When we stay open and curious, we ask ourselves, "What if . . . ?" in a playful, lighthearted way, so that we can remain spontaneous and open to unexpected things that happen. Having a sense of wonder benefits us because we remain curious instead of believing we know everything under the sun.

I learned this hard lesson when I was about 23 years old. I was married to my first husband and had just had my first child. Wanting to stay home during my daughter's formative years, I took a job as an apartment leasing agent and renovation coordinator for a large apartment community that had 230 units. It was a wonderful opportunity for me to meet with adults daily, use my talents, and still be with my daughter all day, as I lived on the site for the first year.

One of my goals was to take the occupancy level up from 82% to 98% by not only acting as general contractor for the property renovation, but also weeding out what the company said were undesirable tenants. They described an undesirable tenant as someone who had an old rusted car in the parking lot, someone who broke the apartment community rules, or someone who didn't pay rent on time.

One Sunday afternoon, when I was holding an open house in the model apartment, a man came in and began walking through the unit. He looked rather grungy, with tattered clothes and dirty hands. I immediately thought about what I had learned in training. *Does he have a rusted old car too?* I wondered. After briefly greeting him, I looked out the patio door window to see if an old rusted car was parked in the visitors' spot in front of the model apartment.

Sure enough, there it was! Quickly coming to judgment about him, in my fear of not meeting my goal, I cut the conversation short and paid more attention to the well-groomed gentleman and his wife who had suddenly entered the model apartment. I excused myself from the grungy man, invited him to look around on his own, and, when he was leaving, thanked him for visiting us.

The next Monday morning, I got a call from my boss. He said, "I heard the owner came to see you Saturday." Not understanding what he was talking about, I inquired, "What do you mean?"

He said, "You know, that guy who came to visit you on Sunday at your open house was the owner."

Amazed at what he was telling me, I asked, "Are you talking about the man who came in with the tattered shorts? The man driving the old rusted car?" He confirmed, in fact, that the man I was describing was the owner-the man I had secretly judged as a bad prospect. All I could think was, *Oh no, I didn't know!* I told myself that I couldn't possibly have known, that I had only been working at the company for a few weeks and had never met the owner, so I shouldn't feel bad.

When I shared my surprise with my boss, I explained that the owner's tattered and dirty clothing and rusty car threw me off. "I was afraid to rent to an undesirable tenant," I said. He laughed and explained that the owner had been working on his Porsche that day and was using his little brother's car so that he could stop by and see how the renovation was going!

Although my mistake didn't get me into trouble with my employer, it was certainly a wake-up call for me. I thought about how quickly I'd taken the advice to prejudge people because of my own fear of renting to the wrong person. My fear of failure caused me to rush to judgment instead of simply considering the signs of an undesirable tenant to be just a general guideline. I missed a prime opportunity to make a good impression on the building owner because I didn't let myself become curious and open to all the many reasons that a man might drive a rusted car and wear tattered clothing.

Although knowing your standards and bottom line
is a good thing, be careful to not be quick to judge.
Instead, look beyond the surface and notice
the world around you.
Be curious . . . and you might be surprised
at what you discover.

BECAUSE WE HAVE STOPPED BEING CURIOUS, WE HAVE A LIMITED VIEW OF OURSELVES AND THE WORLD AROUND US.

Curiosity allows us to visit the unlimited possibilities of ourselves and the world around us. Although it can be a good thing to have a vision for our life and goals that can help us make our dreams come true, we would find life a lot less stressful if we could only stay open to the possibilities that might help lead us to our desired destination. Curiosity can help us do just that.

As we let go of form and hold on to our curiosity, we become more self-aware and see the possibilities around us. As we become more curious, we become more aware of who we are and what we are called to do as life is unfolding in sometimes unexpected ways. When we are connected to our curiosity, we witness how life brings us clues about what we are supposed to do next. When we are not connected to our curiosity, we begin to recognize that the moments in which we didn't choose to love ourselves well were because we didn't even know we had abandoned ourselves. In our blindness to the opportunities that were set before us, we missed out on the more effortless path to reach our goals. Therefore, finding this piece to the personal leadership puzzle can be very freeing and empowering.

Often, when we aren't living the life we expected to live, we believe that someone or even God himself betrayed us. In actuality, we betrayed ourselves because we didn't stay open and curious enough to listen to our inner self that was trying to wake us up and help us become aware of all the opportunities in front of us. It is we who abandoned and betrayed ourselves by not getting curious enough about how we felt or what we needed in a given situation.

When my youngest child was just seven years old, I suddenly discovered that I needed to get curious about what my possibilities were. I was running my own business and working part-time so that I could be available for the kids when they went off to school and home for them when they got back at 4:00 P.M. One day, my husband announced that he wanted a divorce. When I realized that there was no saving the marriage, I instantly panicked, believing I would either have to work full-time and leave my kids to fend for themselves before and after school, or I would have to move and give up the lifestyle we were accustomed to living.

As I shared my fears with others, they reinforced them. I would hear things like, "Well, life is about choices. I guess you will have to choose one or the other-being with your kids or having enough money to stay in your home." That wasn't very comforting, nor did it ring true for me. In my heart, I felt there had to be more possibilities.

I went for a visit down to Florida to see my mom and spend a few days on the beach relaxing as much as I could, hoping that maybe an idea would come to me. It wasn't until I got curious, the first necessary piece in the personal leadership puzzle, that I could see the possibilities beyond my limited thinking. While lying on the beach, I heard a voice from inside of me say, "Go talk to the radio stations in Milwaukee and barter your services. Then you'll spread the word about your business all around town and still be able to support your family in the lifestyle you are accustomed to living."

I knew that my curiosity was keeping me open, and that as a result, I was being guided on what to do next. I remembered how I had a lot of radio experience, as promotion director of a radio station, when I was younger. So I remained open and curious and got the idea to approach the local jazz station, offering to train their sales people if they would pay me half in cash and the rest in commercials to market my business. Sure enough, my "Performance Tips" show aired on their radio station and one thing led to the other. I was getting new business, referrals, and a request from another radio station to actually do a full one-hour talk show on "Performance Solutions."

Being open and curious allowed me to continue living the lifestyle I was accustomed to and to make progress towards my goals, even though my life was taking a form different than I had expected. In spite of the unexpected twist in the road that I came upon when my marriage ended, tapping in to my curiosity allowed me to expand my life and my limited view, and live a complete life.

Embrace your curiosity and expand your view of yourself and the world around you.

WHEN WE STOP ALLOWING OURSELVES TO BE CURIOUS, IT IS BECAUSE WE ARE CARRYING AROUND IN OUR MINDS OLD SCRIPTS ABOUT WHO WE ARE, WHO OTHERS ARE, AND WHAT THE WORLD AROUND US IS LIKE.

Working with organizations on strategic planning, I often notice that people carry around old scripts about how to lead their lives and their organizations. The old, rigid ideas contained in those scripts hold them back from possibilities. And although it is good to take the time to think out our vision, goals, and strategies, if we are to grow, we must go beyond relying on our mind's current ideas and become curious and open to possibilities that haven't occurred to us.

As a life coach, I have heard countless stories of how people are still carrying around old scripts from the past instead of being curious about who they are now and what they want out of their future. Old scripts often include things like rigid ideas about how women are and should be (or how men are or should be), what roles we think we ought to play, or a specific way to go about something that we believe is the correct way to do it. The ideas in these scripts may be very old, left over from criticism that has created emotional scars and from other people who imposed their beliefs on us instead of encouraging us to discover for ourselves what is important to us.

When I work with individuals and businesses in their development, I remind them of the need to work off of a blank piece of paper daily instead of an old script. Although it can be helpful to envision one's life and map it out, we need to hold on to the vision tightly and the map loosely, because roadblocks and detours often show up along the way. We benefit greatly from remaining open and curious and not filling in the blank piece of paper too quickly. Getting curious, although it may seem like it takes time, actually helps us to reach our destination in a timely and effortless way.

When I think of hanging on to old scripts, I am reminded of a client whom I worked with many years ago. He took over his father's business and struggled for years to find his identity and his own way of doing things. His father was a natural people person, demonstrative and loved by his employees. He had a way of making people feel important and cared for, but had a real weakness when it came to managing the day-to-day profitability of the company.

When my client took over his father's business, he felt that he had to somehow fill his father's shoes in the eyes of the employees. Not only did he feel the pressure to be well liked and well received, he also felt the added pressure of meeting the company's new strategic plan and goals so that it could be more profitable.

Feeling this pressure at first caused him to act as if he were his dad, and then, when he wasn't in front of the employees, he would revert back to his more detail-oriented, bottom-line self. After a few years of this chameleon-type of behavior, he came to me feeling exhausted and empty, and confused about what he should do.

After I'd asked him several provocative questions about his relationship with his employees and his beliefs about himself as an employer, he became curious about what had occurred in his company. He soon recognized how he had stopped being curious about what he needed to do and say at work and, instead, was living by a business script. Although he was meeting many of the goals he had set out for the company, he was feeling incomplete. He was growing weary and becoming afraid that he would not be able to continue at this pace without a renewed energy.

To get him back on track, I helped him reconnect with his

childlike wonder and curiosity. We began to do an exercise I call "just imagine." I asked him,

Just imagine...if you were to have started this business years ago, what is the first thing you would have done with it?
Just imagine...that it is ten years from now and that you have the business of your dreams, what are you doing? What are you making? How does it feel?
Just imagine...that you are really connected with your employees. How are you feeling? How are you showing up with them?

As I guided him through these questions, he began to let go of the old scripts he thought he needed to hold on to and began tapping in to his own curiosity and the wonder of his own life instead.

Within six months, he was creating a whole new business, one that was allowing him to feel complete. He was also connecting to his employees in a way that was much more authentic for him given who he is. Instead of trying to connect with his employees in a more personal way, as his father might have done, he held regular strategic sessions, helping his employees to tackle their weekly issues and solve their problems, empowering them to meet their goals. Like the man in this situation, many people get stuck feeling they have to fulfill the role of their predecessor, whether on the job or in a relationship and feeling inauthentic when they do so. Letting go of these old scripts and becoming curious helps us to feel complete.

Map out your vision for your life and your goals.
Hold on to them loosely by revising them regularly.
When you do, take out a new, blank piece of paper. With curiosity and wonder, ask yourself, "Who am I today?" and "How might I go about creating the life I want, right now?"

WE DON'T SEE A CLEAR PATH TO THE VICTORY OF LIVING A COMPLETE LIFE, BECAUSE WE HAVEN'T BECOME CURIOUS ABOUT THE LESSONS OF OUR PAST THAT COULD PROPEL US FORWARD.

Sometimes, it's not the old scripts others give us that bog us down and keep us from leading a complete life. Sometimes, it's what we haven't learned from our past that holds us back. Not learning from our past keeps us falling into the same old hole, because we have a blind spot. Once we fall into the same old hole again, hopefully, we'll start to wonder, *How did I get here anyway?*

To stop falling into the same old self-sabotaging patterns, you need to get curious about the lessons of your past so that you can propel yourself forward. Becoming curious about the part you play in your decisions frees you from choosing self-sabotaging patterns. When you make choices that honor your real self and the vision and goals you have for your life, you will feel complete.

This was true in my life when it came to relationships. I was attracted to charming, demonstrative, and engaging individuals who, at a heart level, were actually quite remote and distant. Although they would reel me in quickly, the depth of the connection rarely went beyond the infatuation stage, leaving me hungry for their curiosity about who I really was at my essence. When I would try to connect more deeply, or become curious about who they were, I often would feel resistance and deception. That prevented us from achieving a mutually loving partnership where both people could grow together in unconditional love and become deeply emotionally intimate.

I realized that if I wanted to heal this self-sabotaging pattern in my life, I needed to become more open and curious about how this tendency to choose such men developed in me. I would have to discover what I was telling myself about myself that led me to choose this type of relationship. As I became curious, I discovered a secret I carried deep within myself that had me convinced that I was not worthy of being unconditionally loved. This belief about myself came from the limited perception I had developed as a result of my busy and hectic childhood, which left me feeling alone, dismissed, and unworthy. Later in life, out of hunger for a close connection, I misinterpreted others' charm as indicating a sincere interest to grow more emotionally connected, when in fact, it did not. Disappointed over and over again, I told myself, "The problem must be me. I am not worthy of love."

It's funny how we will create self-fulfilling prophecies. We would rather be right, and continue to live in our comfort zone of what we believe to be true, than challenge that truth with our own curiosity.

Becoming curious about our self-sabotaging patterns allows us to learn from our past and to see a clear victory in our future. In my particular situation, if I truly wanted a relationship that would be more emotionally intimate, I would have to forego the instant gratification that resulted from staying in my comfort zone. Instead, I'd have to focus on really getting to know someone, becoming emotionally vulnerable, and sharing myself without holding back. I recognized that doing this was scary for me. Choosing to open up emotionally created a space for all of my self-doubt and low self-worth to come out, but once it was out, I'd have a chance to heal it. It also created a space for me to begin to make different choices when men wanted to move quickly in a relationship with me. I started setting boundaries that would give me the space to really know myself-and, as time went on, to really know them, too.

Doubting whether or not I could or would be loved if

someone really knew me, I somehow found the courage to get curious and that allowed me to discover what I thought was so difficult to love about myself. I became increasingly aware of how my own perfectionism was the root cause for me not being able to attract an authentic, loving relationship. I began to transform my own pattern by taking the time to get to know myself, becoming curious about how I felt in situations and what I wanted and needed, and how I might make decisions that were for my highest good. As part of this loving effort, I began to just observe my feelings and needs, without reservation or judgment.

Loving myself in this way, like a loving parent would do, allowed me to propel myself forward and create deeper, more open and honest relationships with other people, including my clients. There were times when I did share my feelings, needs, and boundaries, and they weren't well received. Sometimes, clients and friends rejected me, took things personally, or criticized me for who I was. In those cases, I discovered, I could just observe our differences and their need to judge, and go ahead and make the best decision for myself. Often times, in those cases, I just had to remind myself that I am lovable.

Curiosity will lead us to dig deep down inside into the lies that we told ourselves about ourselves when others did not love us in the way that we needed to be loved. Because we are made for love and connection, we often settle for counterfeit love and admiration instead of insisting upon unconditional love. It is only when we adopt a humble spirit and wake up to the lessons of our past patterns that we can move on to lead a complete life and choose differently in the future.

If we can reflect on past experiences and patterns, with curiosity, we can more easily view others with empathy and compassion when they are stuck in their own self-defeating patterns. We don't necessarily have to tell them what we think their patterns are, but by becoming curious, we signal to them that we are approachable and accepting, and this may give them the courage to become curious themselves.

Being open and curious invites others into a deeper conversation, allowing them to uncover the secret questions lurking within them, such as, "Am I 'enough'? Am I lovable just as I am?" Unless we have gotten curious and done our own personal inventory of our past lessons, we might never know the secret pain others feel. Until we have recognized our own "mask," we cannot recognize the mask that others use to hide their insecurities.

One of the most common masks is having a life filled with people and things that distract us from what we really desire deep down. When we are trying to fill our own void, we seek more: more relationships, more money, more success, more kids, more houses, more cars, etc. We use this mask of "more" to cover an incomplete life, but the mask never fully disguises our sadness, pain, or emptiness.

When we have become curious enough to heal the wounds and patterns of our past, we are able to assist others in getting curious enough to heal their patterns as well. This is true because our empathy assists us in approaching them with more compassion.

Become curious about the lessons of your past. Discover the lie you are holding about yourself that tells you that you are not enough, just as you are. When you do this, you will propel yourself forward and feel complete once again.

BECOMING INWARDLY CURIOUS, AWARE, AND MINDFUL HELPS US HAVE A WIDER PERSPECTIVE.

When we let curiosity help us receive guidance on how to live in each moment, we grow in our ability to honor ourselves and then see and understand the bigger picture. Curiosity helps us to discover not only what feels good in the moment to us, but also the deeper aspects of ourselves, such as our own personal set of values.

Everyone belongs to different groups that have their own set of values. These groups might include:

- *Society*, which tells us that our worth lies in our title, our possessions, and the amount of money we have.
- *Church*, which tells us how we should behave in our relationships with others.
- *Parents*, who teach us to value what they think is important.
- *Co-workers*, including bosses and supervisors and those we supervise, who tell us to live according to their standard of acceptable behavior.
- *Community*, which lets us know what we have to do to be accepted.
- *Friends*, who show us through their behavior how to act in order to be loved.

There is no doubt that we are constantly being bombarded with messages about how to act in any given situation if we are concerned about being safe, secure, loved, and part of a group.

Becoming more inwardly curious, aware, and mindful of your own thoughts, feelings, needs, and values allows you to make your own choices and avoid falling into "group think." As you become more curious about and mindful of who you are and the choices before you, you'll stop feeling as if you're a victim of circumstance.

Even when you make a point of being curious about yourself and mindful of your thoughts, feelings, needs, and values, sometimes you will make choices you'll later regret. Hindsight is 20/20, but it's only natural that you'll sometimes make choices that produce results you don't like. When this happens, be grateful for the opportunity to learn what the experience has to teach you, learn the lesson, and move on.

By leading your life in this loving way, you will allow curiosity to help you discover who you are as well as your own personal value system and the goals you have for your life. You'll become a curious observer of your environment, your thoughts, your sensations, and your choices along the way.

One of the most important things to be mindful about is the foundation for your decision making. To become mindful, ask yourself, "Am I making choices out of fear of the outcome? Or, am I making choices out of love for myself, including the vision I have for my life, my value system, and my goals?" If you are making choices out of fear, stop focusing on your "not goal," the place you hope not to arrive at, and start focusing on your positive, desired goal instead. If you find this to be difficult, then start getting curious again. Ask yourself, "What is it that I want for my life, in this particular area of my life?" and discover your positive goal.

Often, we know what we do not want, but we don't know what we want. That is because most of us have spent more time in our fear than in our curiosity.

Begin focusing on what you want by becoming curious
about the choices that caused you to abandon
and betray yourself in the past.
Then, commit to being inwardly curious,
aware, and mindful in the present moment
so that you can lead a complete life!

WE CAN REPLACE OUR FEAR, SELF-DOUBT, AND CONFUSION WITH CURIOSITY.

Sometimes, we just wake up and for no particular reason, we feel out of sorts. One day, we can feel on top of our game, while another day, inexplicably, we are struck by all sorts of inhibiting feelings such as fear, self-doubt, and confusion. In fact, the Institute of Psychiatry in London says that at any given time, 3 to 5 percent of adults suffer from generalized daily anxiety or depression.

When you're feeling out of sorts and anxious, curiosity can lead you back to feeling like yourself again. Instead of getting so busy that you are completely distracted from your feelings, how about trying something different? How about becoming clearer, by connecting with yourself more deeply, instead?

I encourage my clients to learn how to connect with themselves in a loving and nurturing way, so that they can discover what they need and feel. I ask them to think back to when they were a child and experienced a bad day at school, a time when that they felt scared, sad, and confused. I ask them to identify the source of their negative feelings-a bad grade on a test, another child teasing them, a teacher criticizing them, and so on.

Next, I have them conjure up an imaginary parent, one that would have been so in tune with them emotionally that they would've noticed their child's unhappiness the moment the child walked in the door after school. I tell them to imagine that this parent would ask, "How was your day? You seem sad," and if you denied that you had a difficult day, they would know, and encourage you to talk about it.

I continue and ask them to further imagine this parent as being extremely wise: a parent who does not live out of fear of what might happen if they can't fix their child's problem, or begin making judgments about what might have caused this bad day (such as that you didn't apply yourself, or the teacher was unfair, and so on). Instead, this parent would be open and curious enough to guide you, without judgment, to explore what had happened. He or she would help you to receive wisdom and love, and to trust that the answers will come to you in perfect timing.

Usually at this point, most people say, "That wasn't how either of my parents acted!" Although many people came from loving homes where their daily needs were met and they were provided safety and security, most of the people I know are able to begin to recognize that their parents were not as emotionally available as they needed them to be.

Once this recognition occurs, I ask them to forgive their parents for not knowing how to emotionally nurture them at times. I also ask them to let go of being stuck in that situation by seeing clearly in their mind's eye a new, emotionally available parent who wants to assist them through difficult times, whenever they need love, acceptance, and guidance. I tell them that this loving parent will be there to guide them through their fear, self-doubt, and confusion by staying alongside of them as they become curious.

Then I ask them to again go back and imagine that difficult day at school and, this time, imagine that they are sitting alongside their imaginary parent, who is kind, open, and curious. The imaginary parent asks them good, open-ended questions about their day. I ask them to imagine the conversation going something like this:

"See your mother sitting alongside of you on your bed or the living room sofa. Imagine her softness, her approachability, and her interest in what you are feeling and needing. Now imagine yourself feeling open, safe, and connected. When she asks you about your day, know that she is only trying to get you to become more mindful of your fear, self-doubt, and confusion so that you can face your difficult situation. Allow yourself to see this more fearful and insecure part of yourself with the same unconditional love that your mother is offering you right now. Now, as you see your difficult situation, imagine your mother asking you what you need to do or say to feel better and more complete. Wait in the stillness for the answer to come to you. Be patient and trusting, waiting until you can hear the voice within, guiding you to know what to do or say. Feel your patience and the patience of your loving parent, who trusts and allows wisdom to come in perfect timing. Stay with your parent in that stillness. Feel the comforting energy that allows you to feel complete right now. Feel the joy and delight this parent has in you, just as you are. Feel yourself in touch with your essence once again."

As I do this exercise with my clients, I remind them that part of mindfulness is recognizing when we need to nurture ourselves back to completeness. We can assist ourselves in transforming out of our fear, self-doubt and confusion by asking ourselves loving questions.

Loving questions sound like:

"*How was your day today?*"

"*How did that make you feel?*"

"*Why was that hard (or wonderful) for you?*"

"*What do you think you need to do or say to feel complete right now?*"

> *Love yourself and engage in an inner dialog of curiosity regularly in order to help bring you back to feeling complete once again.*

LIKE SCIENTISTS, WE CAN BECOME CURIOUS,

RECITING THE MANTRA,

"HMM . . . ISN'T THAT INTERESTING? I WONDER . . ."

As we live in the wonder of life, we find ourselves thinking much like a scientist. We step back and observe situations and human nature with an inquisitive eye, an open heart, and a curious mind. Although we begin to see patterns and start to notice how things fit together, we are careful to not draw conclusions too easily. Instead, we realize the importance of staying open and curious.

The way this process works is that first, when you notice something that feels confusing or uncomfortable for you, you slow down that mad, mental rush to judgment and negative conclusions by saying to yourself:

"Hmm..."

This could happen when you ask someone a direct question and the answer does not match your perception of the person's mood. Then, when you notice another sign that tells you that you hunch about what is really going on might be correct, you might say to yourself:

"Hmm . . . isn't that interesting (that person does seem upset even though she is saying that she is not)..."

This statement allows you to be more open to your curiosity. Then, the third time you notice something that appears to validate your hunch, you say to yourself:

"Hmm . . . isn't that interesting? I wonder what that is about (I wonder what the other person is upset about and why she does not want to talk about it or acknowledge it)?"

This thought takes you further into the possibilities that don't always come quickly to mind because of your knee-jerk responses and old mental patterns that have gone unquestioned.

Just as a scientist would first observe her subject and then form a hypothesis, so, too, does the curious mind observe life and then experience hunches. Hunches are those gut feelings we get when our subconscious mind has been watching out for us and observing what it is we are interested in, so that we take conscious notice and pause.

Unfortunately, however, once we wake up to what is going on around us and inside us, pausing and staying in a sense of wonder can be difficult. Staying open and aware can be especially difficult if you only have a stop-and-go sign and are not in touch with your flashing yellow light within that tells you to slow down and yield-yield to the process of allowing wisdom to come to you in its own time. The reason many of us have not developed this yellow light is that our ego likes to be right and in control, so pausing in the unknown feels uncomfortable. We want the answers, and we want them right now! We would rather be in or out of a situation or relationship than sit in a waiting room and wonder about what might happen.

When yielding and observing is difficult for you, you can practice staying in curiosity and developing your ability to be comfortable when the yellow light is flashing and asking you to yield. A great way to get comfortable with uncertainty, and to practice your curiosity, is by doing a One-Minute Meditation.

THE ONE-MINUTE MEDITATION

First, prepare by detaching from the person you're with, or the situation you're in by saying:

"Hmm . . . isn't that interesting? I wonder . . ."
(Finish the sentence with whatever it is that you are wondering about-why the person is angry, why he seems to be dodging your question, etc.)

This statement helps you to yield and puts you in a neutral, observant state of mind. Simply feel curious and observe the behavior or situation around you without judgment. You're being judgmental when you conclude someone or something is good or bad, or right or wrong.

Now, become open and connect with your curiosity by saying:

"I am able to attract truth and wisdom in perfect timing."

This affirmation opens you up to your inner guidance and connects you with your heart, which is where you know truth and love.

Continue to be curious and connect with yourself by taking three deep, cleansing breaths. As you breathe in, picture yourself breathing in peace and love. As you exhale, picture yourself exhaling anxiety and fear.

Now that you're in a neutral and observant state of being, yielding to your situation, you are ready to access the scientist within you who loves to observe with curiosity. You can do this with what I call the Six-Point Check. The Six-Point Check enables you to observe, without judgment, what you are noticing in the world around you, as well as the inner world within you. It takes you one step deeper into your curiosity and observation.

THE SIX-POINT CHECK

First, notice what's happening in the world around you by asking:

- **Point 1**: What am I hearing them say?
- **Point 2**: What am I seeing them do?
- **Point 3**: What am I sensing from their emotional energy?

(Asking these questions raises your level of awareness, openness, and curiosity about the world around you.)

Now go into the last three points of the Six-Point Check, noticing what is going on within you. Ask yourself,

- **Point 4**: What am I hearing the small voice within myself say?
- **Point 5**: What am I seeing in my mind's eye?
- **Point 6**: What am I sensing in my body/emotions?

(Asking these questions raises your level of awareness, openness, and curiosity about the world inside of you.)

Practicing the One-Minute Meditation and the Six-Point Check will help you achieve the first piece of the personal leadership puzzle, which is to get curious. Being open and curious will help you to find the next piece: get clear.

Become an open and curious observer of yourself and your world by saying, "Hmm . . . isn't that interesting? I wonder . . . "

SECOND PIECE:

GET CLEAR! SLOW DOWN TO SEE BEYOND THE FOG

Becoming clear means we have become curious and let go of confusion, become more discerning, and started to perceive truth more easily. The transformation from confusion to clarity comes from listening to what our mind, eyes, ears, heart, gut feelings, and spiritual knowing tell us. When we combine information from all of these sources, we are able to trust ourselves more. Getting clear allows us to be more certain of our values and our goals, and make decisions in accordance with them.

Becoming clear is a result of slowing down, taking note, and letting go of our attachments to things like safety and security and feeling loved and accepted. Instead of focusing on attaining something outside of ourselves, we become more aware of how important it is to make decisions that allow us to be true to ourselves. Being clear helps us to free ourselves from the limitations of our mind and know what is real and true for us. When we have a clear mind, we are able to be discerning.

BEFORE WE CAN LIVE A FULFILLED, COMPLETE LIFE,

WE MUST GET CLEAR.

Becoming clear and self-aware is the second piece in the personal leadership puzzle. To become clear and self-aware means living consciously. It requires that you take a regular inventory of your life, your thoughts, your feelings, and your needs so that you can make responsible choices according to your unique set of values and goals.

So what keeps us from becoming clear? Instead of slowing down to get clear about our likes, dislikes, and values, and ensuring that we are making choices to meet our goals, we choose to subscribe to group think. We live in a society where great value is placed on belonging, and where finding one's true self is not emphasized. In fact, we often call people who are true to themselves "selfish," shaming them back into submission so that they'll be a more cooperative team member, friend, family member, or co-worker. Rather than acting "selfishly," we ignore the abundance of wisdom within and try to conform to how others think and feel.

Even when we do dare to go within to begin our personal leadership journey, ignoring the external voices, we face these same people within the voices in our head. We hear internal voices that tell us we are being foolish to act differently from how others expect us to behave.

What keeps us from fulfillment and effectiveness is not those external and internal voices but our own fears and self-doubts that stem from our deep need to belong and to feel safe and secure. We are afraid to quiet our minds and listen within, because we know that time and time again, as we try to get clear, we will have to face the chatter in our head, the thumping in our heart, and the knot in our stomach.

Learning to slow down and be clear will help you to make choices that will bring about the changes you envision. It will allow you to face your resistance and your need for safety, security, love, and belonging.

Start having a love affair with yourself. Slow down enough to hear what you need and how you feel.
Honor yourself and you will begin to feel complete.

IF YOU DO NOT HEAR WITHIN YOU AN ANSWER TO YOUR QUESTION, STAY OPEN TO RECEIVE WISDOM SO THAT YOU CAN BECOME CLEAR IN PERFECT TIMING.

The hardest part about slowing down to get clear is when we slow down but we don't get clear right away. We are used to instant gratification and high-tech speed, so when information isn't coming to us right away, we begin to feel frustrated and impatient. Then we begin to doubt that there really is any wisdom within us.

Slowing down to get clear is like going to the gym to build muscles-it doesn't happen overnight. We have to be consistent and gradually build up our strength and endurance. Only then do we begin to see results.

At other times, when we ask a question and we still don't hear anything, it is because the timing is not right. This happened to me recently when I slowed down, got clear, and waited for an answer about my office space dilemma. For two years, I had been unhappy with the new owners of the space I was renting due to the changes they were making about billing, policies, and equipment. Although the space had served me well for 12 years, it no longer was working for me. I began envisioning having an office in a building on a lake. I was clear about what the building would look like, where I wanted it to be, what I felt comfortable paying for the space, and the feeling I wanted my clients to experience when they were there. Because I was so clear about what I wanted, I expected that it would show up soon, but for years I couldn't find the right property to buy or rent. Because I was unhappy in my office space, I kept wondering what I should do. Was there something I wasn't seeing?

Then one day, I confronted the owner of my building about

some of the changes he had made and the mistakes that kept showing up on my bills. Within 24 hours, I received a short-term eviction notice. Although I had slowed down and gotten clear about my situation, being thrown into the unknown in this way was not what I had hoped for or expected. I had thought I would get a clear answer, not an unexpected order to move immediately!

That afternoon, I drove home from the office and decided to take the scenic beachfront drive home instead of my usual highway route. As I passed the downtown beach and storefronts, which were only one mile from my house, I noticed a sign on one of the windows that said, "Office For Rent." I was surprised because my daughters and I had walked this path many times and previously saw a sign in the same window that simply said, "For Rent." We assumed it was a retail space, since the eight buildings all had retail businesses and restaurants in them. In fact, I had remembered joking with the girls about what a great location it was and that we ought to think of a business we could have there, like a breakfast and coffee spot, just to take advantage of the terrific space and gorgeous location.

Realizing what was for rent was actually office space, I immediately felt hopeful once again and called the phone number on the sign. To my surprise, the rent amount was comparable to what I was currently paying. After looking at the space, I could see that, although I had been asking, "What should I do about my office space?" for two years, I wasn't meant to receive an answer until everything had lined up in perfect timing. What a nice gift this was, especially since I had just moved to a home less than a mile away a couple of months before! It was a great reminder that we don't control the timing of the solutions and answers that come to us, but they do come to us.

Get clear and stay open to receive wisdom in perfect timing.

AS WE BECOME MORE CLEAR ABOUT THE MOMENT-TO-MOMENT CHOICES IN OUR LIVES, WE ARE BETTER ABLE TO EFFORTLESSLY REACH OUR FINAL DESTINATION.

Self-awareness allows us to notice the moment-to-moment opportunities for leading a more complete life. It is the mini-moments of choice that determine where we end up and who we end up with in our lives. If we are not feeling complete, we need to reevaluate our choices so that they are aligned with our values, our goals, and our needs.

As I life coached a woman who, like me, had been married several times, I could hear in her story echoes of other stories I'd heard. She was in yet another marriage where she was feeling more alone than she had been when she was single. In all of these cases, the relationship started out with fiery infatuation but once this stage was over, unresolved conflict made it difficult for her or her partner to breathe around each other. Because they were not able to be emotionally intimate and communicate clearly with one another, each person felt they had to lose a part of themselves in order to be in the relationship.

Looking back at her relationship patterns, she admitted that infatuation propelled her forward, and that she never really took the time to explore any of her partners, or her dynamic with them, in any depth before committing to a relationship. In fact, when there were red flags early on, she dismissed them and told herself that love would conquer all and "This is as good as it gets."

That very week, I had done business coaching at a workplace and heard a similar story. I'd been coaching a manager of a small company and she was frustrated about an employee she had just hired who had sounded terrific in her initial interview but now was not putting the needed energy into her job. Just like my client who was struggling with marital issues, this client was also feeling confusion and hopelessness.

In both cases, I could see a common pattern. Both people admitted in hindsight that they had not stuck with their bottom-line nor listened to their instincts along the way. They rationalized away their inner knowing by saying to themselves things such as, "You are asking too much," "You won't find something better," "It's a tough world out there and the pickings are slim," "You can't have everything," "This is as good as it gets," and "I can work with this person and change him/her."

Settling for less in the hope that you'll arrive where you want to go more quickly can actually, in the long run, delay your arrival. If this is the case for you, learn from your past and slow down so that you can make different moment-to-moment choices that honor your inner knowing and make you feel more clear and thus more complete.

To change the pattern of abandoning your values, slow down and get clear about how you dismiss your feelings and needs. This will help you to be more clear as you make your moment-to-moment choices.

WE OFTEN MISINTERPRET OUR TOUGH EXPERIENCES IN LIFE. THE TRUTH IS, THEY ARE GIVEN TO US TO HELP US GET CLEAR ABOUT OUR CALLING.

I'll never forget one day when I was about 16 years old, my aunt, who was the president of a local Catholic college, said to me, “"Have you heard the calling?"

I wasn't certain what she meant. I looked at her in her nun outfit and thought, "Surely she doesn't think I want to be a nun, does she?"

Looking at her, a bit concerned, I said, "No, not really. I don't think that I want to be a nun. That's not for me."

She smiled and said, "No, I mean *your* calling."

Without further explanation, she let it go, knowing she had planted a seed for my growth. Months later, I heard the calling she was talking about when I was watching Leo Buscaglia on PBS speaking about love. As he was speaking, something resonated in my heart, and I knew that I, too, wanted to be an author and speaker on love someday. I remembered the seed my aunt had planted in my heart and mind about becoming clear about my calling. When I next saw her, I told her that I did hear my calling; I just wasn't sure how I was going to achieve my goal.

In her affirming and clear way, my aunt said to me, "You'll know. It will come to you a step at a time, as you need."

This awareness of and clarity about my calling was one of the best things that ever happened to me. Although I learned about my calling early in my life, it was the difficulties in my life that clarified the truth about my calling. These experiences also brought a richness to my speaking and writing that education alone could not.

Because I had struggled in my younger years with feeling

unlovable and believed it was because of circumstances like my parents getting a divorce and my mother often being physically and emotionally unavailable, I could empathize later in life with people who also believed that something outside of them caused their painful feelings and the difficult circumstances they were in. Just like many people who haven't yet realized that it is our thoughts about ourselves and our choices that create our circumstances, I searched outside of myself for someone or something to make me feel better about who I was.

It wasn't until I became aware of this tendency to abandon myself and give my power away for the sake of validation that I could learn how to love myself and stay within my center, no matter what anyone else was choosing to do, say, or feel about me. Now, whether I am with or without a partner or a perfect job, or I have someone difficult to deal with, I feel complete and lovable, because I now believe I AM lovable. Because of this transformation experience, I have found my calling, which is to help others to transform their own feelings of low self-worth so that they can be clear about the wonder of who they are.

Let your tough experiences act as a clue to your calling. Slow down and get clear about what emotions you are experiencing and the lies you hold about yourself that lurk deep beneath the surface. Although often we don't want to face and feel these undesirable beliefs and emotions, we can learn how to be comfortable if we just practice and then quickly transform the old feelings and beliefs. As we realize that our experiences and emotions are there to inform us of the lessons of the tough experiences in our past, we will find our calling.

Don't let tough times get you down.
See them differently. Ask, "How might this experience help me get clear about my calling?"

SLOWING DOWN HELPS US GET CLEAR ON A MOMENT-TO-MOMENT BASIS, INCREASING OUR DISCERNMENT, AT WORK AND AT HOME.

Sometimes, it is easy to see how the pieces of our life fit together, while at other times, we can't see it at all. Certain experiences provide sharper images, just like puzzle pieces that have obvious edges or big, bold colors. We look at a situation in our life and know just how it fits into the overall picture. But then there are the other pieces that we are not sure about. What do we do with them?

When we don't slow down enough to get clear and be discerning, we can fall into the trap of making ineffective decisions for ourselves. Discernment is keenness of insight and good judgment and it helps us to make good decisions for ourselves in every area of our life: physical, emotional, financial, relational, recreational, and so on.

It is difficult to have insight and make good choices when we aren't slowing down enough to hear our own body's signals telling us when we have violated our own value system, feelings, or needs. If we get a headache, we quickly take an aspirin rather than slowing down to get clear. We don't recognize the anger causing the headache, anger that is telling us that something needs to change and that we need to deal with it. If we get a stomachache, we take an antacid when we would probably be better off becoming still and asking ourselves, "What am I concerned about? What is my gut feeling?"

Without knowing our own value system and who we are, how can we possibly be clear and discerning? And for that matter, until we fully understand the relevance of getting clear and being more discerning ourselves, we will continue to give our children quick answers, such as daring them to say no to drugs, when we really should be helping them explore why they are considering taking drugs: Why do they want to belong a particular group of drug-using kids so badly anyway? Having that type of authentic conversation with our children would mean hearing about feelings we might not know how to deal with, because we haven't faced them in ourselves first.

Slowing down to get clear, whether that is with yourself, your employees or co-workers, or your children, will assist you in leading a complete life because you will feel empowered to choose. You will be considering your own needs, feelings, and goals and who you are at your essence. For example, perhaps you have a hard time speaking up when others are angry. By slowing down and becoming self-aware, you can get clear and realize that it is you who may need to get angry instead of staying stuck in fear, so that you can make the changes you need in order to love yourself well in that relationship.

Getting clear and becoming more discerning allows us to make the minor moment-to-moment choices that lead us to more confidently choose the right course for ourselves when faced with major opportunities. Often, we are consumed with finding our calling, when we haven't even heard the little whispering voice asking us to choose our own priorities, needs, and values in the mini-moments before us. How can we accept our calling in life and be so bold as to carry that out if we can't even listen to the whisper in the moment that is guiding us along the way? Surely, if given our calling, we would quickly get off our own path, even if we were to get on it for a moment.

I believe this is why often, people who have had instant success develop addictive behaviors. Perhaps they have not taken the time to get clear enough to see and feel how the instant success has caused much change in their lives. When self-destruction occurs after instant success, it is not the success that caused the problem, but rather the lack of self-awareness that lead to a lack of discernment. It seems that often, the pressure to stay at the top prevents people from breathing, from taking the time to process what has just happened and to discover what it is they want to do next with their lives. I have seen this with clients who have sold their business and quickly jumped into another and with people who I have known who have either inherited money or won the lottery. Moving quickly without taking the time to discover our own needs, priorities, and desires can often led us down the path of impulsivity and regret.

Fine-tuning our discernment begins by living your life each and every moment with more discernment so that you can discover, "Who am I in this moment?" and to ask of yourself, "How might I be discerning, so that I might feel complete?" As you read about this second piece to the personal leadership puzzle, you might instantly feel afraid that we could all become a society of "instant gratifiers." You might think, *If I choose to honor my own values, feelings, and needs in the moment, does that mean that I eat the ice cream I want right now, instead of delaying gratification so that I can fit in the jeans I want to wear later? Or, does that mean I spend the money on something I want now at the mall, only to forfeit the financial comfort of a home I wanted to buy and had been saving for? Do I let the "jerk-at-work" belittle me in front of others, only to quiet my voice because I am afraid of losing my job?*

There is a great difference between making impulsive decisions that contradict our values and take us away from our goals and making decisions that honor what we value. Impulsive decision making may leave us with a high for a short period of time, but this will be followed by regret. When we make impulsive decisions based on short-term, instant gratification instead of our deeper feelings and greater goals, we ruin our chances for feeling complete because we feel bad about ourselves. On the other hand, when we make decisions that honor our values, feelings, and needs, we awaken to our essence and feel fulfilled.

Slowing down will help us arrive at true self-awareness, which will then lead us to being more discerning, because we will be clear about who we are, what we want, and the choices we need to make to help us get there. As we begin to slow down and know ourselves, recognizing what feels good and what feels bad, we develop our own set of personal values and goals.

But slowing down can often be very scary. We believe that time is of the essence, and that time is money, so we do not want to waste time by slowing it down.

If this is what you are struggling with, recognize that fretting over things is, in fact, a waste of time. Slowing down to get clear will ultimately save you time, because you will have a clear path to your destination. By taking the time to get to know your own set of values and goals, you'll be able to be more clear and discerning when making decisions.

Slow down and get clear about your needs, feelings, and values so that you can be more discerning.

INSTEAD OF LIVING OUR LIVES BY OUR OWN INNER GUIDE, WE OFTEN LIVE BY A SET OF INHERITED VALUES, AND THEN WONDER WHY WE ARE NOT CLEAR ABOUT WHAT WE TRULY WANT FOR OURSELVES.

When our mind tells us one thing and our heart tells us another, we become confused instead of clear and discerning. This happens when we hear strong messages from our families, churches, friends, and communities on how we should feel, think, and act in given situations. Because we all like to feel loved and accepted, we often ignore the inner guide telling us what is right for us and instead, we do what we think is acceptable to others. Not being true to our own needs and values leaves us feeling lost, empty, and incomplete. Our fear of disapproval prevents us from getting clear. We're afraid that if we do get in touch with what is most important to us, we'll have to resolve the contradiction between what we want and what others expect of us.

For example, you may have inherited a value system from your church that says that sex outside of marriage is wrong. Perhaps you found yourself contradicting that teaching, and felt guilty and confused. In a situation like this, it's important to slow down, get clear, and be honest with yourself, asking, "What are my values regarding sex outside of marriage?" Or, perhaps you say that your company values integrity and honesty, yet you find yourself manipulating the truth to customers just to keep them, or withholding information from employees so that they won't get scared and leave. Again, this would be a good sign to slow down and notice the contradiction between your words and your behavior. Reserve judgment; just observe yourself.

Often, we say that we embrace certain values but we don't

live by them because something else is more important to us. When you claim to hold a particular value but find yourself contradicting it with your words or actions, it is time to explore yourself more deeply and ask,

"Hmm...isn't that interesting? I wonder, what do I really value?"

<u>Your process of exploration can include</u>:

- Talking about your values with people who you know will honor your individuality.
- Journaling to discover what you truly feel and believe.
- Praying and meditating.
- Working with a life coach or counselor.
- Reading about the topic and gathering more information on it.
- Having different experiences and learning from them.
- Reading the Bible or other spiritual books.

When you are feeling unclear about your deepest feelings and beliefs, you can be honest with yourself and say, "I am not sure where I stand on that topic," and then continue to explore what your values are. It's better to be clear that you are not clear than to be self-deceptive.

Our value system may change as time goes on and we become more self-aware, more aware of information that we might not have possessed before, and we have new experiences. Our values represent where we stand on a particular issue, at a particular time, and may include:

Emotional awareness and honesty with one's self and others

Openness

Honesty

Self-care

Mutually loving relationships

Growth

Physical health

Spiritual connection

Being courageous

Be clear about your values, because they provide an inner compass, helping to guide you in your decision making so that you can feel that your thoughts, feelings, and actions are in alignment.

BEING CLEAR ABOUT YOUR VALUES WILL HELP YOU TO BE CLEAR ABOUT HOW TO GO ABOUT ACHIEVING YOUR GOALS.

Just as our values serve as our compass, our goals serve as our destination. Getting clear about our goals and where we want to be helps us feel more complete because once we know where we want to go, it is easier to get there.

For example, your goals may include:

Physical: Lose ten pounds; decrease high blood pressure.

Intellectual: Write a book; research methods to handle stress.

Emotional: Become more self-aware; honor yourself in decision making; create a peaceful and organized home or office environment.

Spiritual: Slow down and connect to my Divine Source.

Relational: Create mutual, loving, and authentic relationships.

Career: Do more of what I love; create more value and abundance.

Financial: Create wealth without having to work more hours.

Knowing your values and goals will guide you in making choices that lead you to feel complete. At work, you may have a goal to create more abundance but you may value family time. In this case, you may want to do what you can to increase your wealth by creatively thinking of possibilities but not at the expense of working more hours, which would cut into your family time.

Keep in mind, however, that different people may share the

same goals but have different values and priorities. For example, if you value integrity, you may choose to speak up in a relationship more so than someone else who values peace at all costs. Both people could have a goal to build a mutually loving relationship, but their values will cause them to go about building it differently, and perceiving it differently.

Being clear about your values and your goals will help you to make conscious decisions for yourself that honor who you are and what you need. You can then choose the activities that will help you to reach your goals. You will know your priorities and can make decisions that are in alignment with your inner compass and desired destination.

Be clear about your values so that you will be more clear about how to go about achieving your goals.

FEELINGS OF EMPTINESS CAN ACT AS A BRIDGE TO BECOMING CLEAR ABOUT A NEW BEGINNING.

Sometimes when we slow down, we feel an emptiness that can lead us to feeling depressed. Feelings of sadness often accompany emptiness, because we are grieving, emptying ourselves of an identity that no longer fits and making room for a new one. When we take the time to become clear about that emptiness, we enter the void we are experiencing, learn what our situation has to teach us, and discover a reason to move on. Being with our emptiness, we can create something new in this space.

When feeling empty, be careful not to tell yourself additional lies about yourself and your situation that would lead to further anxiety and depression. Beware of self-defeating lies such as, "I am no one without (the kids, the job, the husband)", "I am not worthy, and therefore, I feel this emptiness," "I will never figure this out," "This emptiness feels so bad, I could just die," and "I need (blank) in order to not feel empty." These feelings can propel you downward into a depressive or anxious cycle.

Again, personal leadership requires you to consciously observe your thoughts, feelings, and behaviors. When you can clearly recognize this empty feeling as a bridge to a new beginning, you can say to yourself, "Wow, I am being emptied right now, and my life as I know it is changing. I wonder, what is this empty feeling trying to tell me?" By doing this, you allow yourself to make room for something new to come into your life.

Recognizing the root cause of our emptiness can lead us on an exciting journey of self-love, self-exploration, and self-empowerment. I felt this feeling of emptiness for a period of time the fall of 2005 when my youngest daughter went away to college. I was an empty nester (boy, just thinking of this phrase could make you feel empty!). After 24 years of caring for my two daughters, I was now 46 and alone. I decided that rather than being depressed, I was going to make the most of my new life before me, so I bought a house on the lake. This was a dream come true: I finally had a place to write, relax, and entertain. The only problem was that part of my dream was to be able to share it with my family and a significant other and now I was alone, feeling empty. It seemed the dream was incomplete. Although I had met many wonderful single people in my new lake community, with whom I was having more fun with than I had in years, deep inside, I was still feeling empty.

Rather than deny this emptiness, I decided to become curious about it, and discover what it had to teach me. I slowed down, entered the emptiness within, and discovered a lie that was causing this feeling: the lie that I was not lovable enough to attract a significant other who could unconditionally love me and give to me in a relationship as much as I would give to him. My past had left me believing that I would be dismissed and left alone if I claimed that need, so I had buried it deep inside me. As a result, I believed that in order to connect and keep a relationship, I would have to be the one to continually give, or I would have to be independent and alone. Being clear about this lie helped me to focus on the root cause of my feeling incomplete. It also led me to make different choices right from the start of a potential relationship. Now, I was able to be clear with myself and the man I was with, acting in accordance to the expectations I had of a relationship instead of wasting time being dishonest with myself and with him.

Now that I am more clear about the meaning of this feeling of emptiness that still visits me from time to time, I can make different choices. Instead of trying harder to connect with other people or fill the void inside me with unsatisfying relationships, I slow down to remind myself that I am worthy of a mutually loving relationship.

There are many ways we can try to fill our void: We can choose to be extremely busy, be in an unhealthy relationship, eat too much, drink too much, spend too much, work too much, etc. When we become curious and clear about what we really need to learn in this empty space, we will experience a deeper healing, and feel fulfilled and complete regardless of our circumstances.

Allow the feelings of emptiness to exist.
As you connect with this feeling, you connect with yourself,
thus you will feel complete once again.

SHARPENING YOUR DISCERNMENT AND LIVING YOUR LIFE IN ALPHA HELPS YOU TO GET CLEAR.

"I don't have time to slow down!" This is something I often hear not only from my clients, but also from many people I know socially. Interestingly, when we ask people how they are, they often answer by saying, "Busy!" Listening to this time and time again, I hear an almost sense of pride behind the words. Have we come to believe that being "a busy Beta," caught up at the anxious, gotta-make-the-phone call-and-check-the-e-mail level of consciousness, has actually made us more important? If so, I would question how we are arriving at such a conclusion, especially when busy-ness often leaves us with a feeling of being incomplete, because we are disconnected from ourselves.

On the other hand, living in alpha, the state of being in the flow where we believe we are achieving because we are not experiencing anxiety, allows us to be more clear about what we are thinking, feeling, and needing in any given situation. It is like the difference between taking a super highway home from work versus the slow country road that winds past rivers and fields. In the first case, you are traveling at high speed, looking forward to reach your destination. In the second case, you are headed for your destination but you are also aware of your journey along the way, feeling a greater sense of connection to yourself, your surroundings, and your inner world as you travel.

There are three reasons we believe we don't have enough time for the more connected way to live our lives:

1) **We have filled our lives with too many activities** (fearing that if we don't we will be alone and that will

mean we are a loser. Of course, we wouldn't feel that way if we didn't already believe deep down that we are a loser. Hmm . . . isn't that interesting?).

2) **We get easily distracted.** We may do this because we've gotten into the habit of focusing on what others think and want and have forgotten what we think and want for ourselves. It wouldn't be so hard to focus on our own needs and feelings if we would allow ourselves to feel our own emptiness, explore it, and go deeper into the discovery of ourselves. To do that, we would need to believe we are worth the investment of time. (Hmm . . . isn't that interesting?)

3) **We are perfectionists and waste time** fretting over small matters, insisting that everything has to be perfect and in our control. We could feel more comfortable letting some of these things go if we felt okay about ourselves on the inside and believed that we are "enough" even when our lives get a bit messy. (Hmm . . . isn't that interesting?)

I visited my own issues about slowing down and living in alpha when I was writing this book and exploring the lie within that told me that I always had to be the giver in order to have a loving relationship. Because I was given an opportunity to appear on my local PBS station as part of their funding drive, and needed to get my third book finished in a shorter period of time than I was originally planning, I had very little free time for almost six weeks while I was writing the book. I knew that if I wanted to express myself effectively, I had to get into an alpha state, meaning I would have to cut out distractions, live with imperfection, and be comfortable just sitting in front of the computer at times with no ideas flowing forth. I had to trust that feeling of emptiness that often precedes wisdom.

As I chose to meet the challenging deadline, I was offered an opportunity to develop my own personal leadership. It seems that when I write on a topic, I become increasingly aware of how to live out my book's message. I go beyond intellectual understanding and have an experiential understanding of my ideas. This helps me grow in empathy as well as well as in humility, as I remember that I, too, am still a work in progress!

As I set about finding time in my calendar to focus on writing my book, I was bombarded with phone calls from clients who were anxious and believed they were in need of my coaching services right at that moment. I also seemed to have friends that were in more need of connection for different reasons: They were just starting to break up a relationship, had found out about a sick loved one, were struggling with finances, and so on. Not only was I becoming increasingly aware of the chaos around me, but I was also noticing the chaos within me, as I saw how my environment was becoming unruly. I had laundry all over my bedroom closet floor, unfiled paperwork scattered across my desk, dust building up on the tables, and clutter throughout the house reminding me of my neglect. While this state of disarray caused me some anxiety, the greatest reason for my discomfort was the guilt that was being stirred up inside of me, caused by thoughts that were telling me I should have my house in order even though I was busy at work. Recognizing these thoughts and feelings, I was able to strengthen my ability to get clear and make better moment-to-moment choices that were more in alignment with my deepest desires instead of in alignment with what others might be expecting of me.

As we go deeper into the process of healing and transformation, we are often met with our worst nightmares. It is as if God (or the Universe) is setting up a scenario, so that we have an opportunity to learn a lesson that would help us to live a more complete life. My lesson came when the family down the road decided to stop in unexpectedly one night. They were new in the neighborhood and my daughter had just baked them cookies as a way to welcome them. We were supposed to stop by at their new house to drop them off but, instead, they decided to just come over on their way home from a meeting, without calling first. Noticing that I had redecorated my living room, and knowing that I had planned to do a lot of renovations in my house, their curiosity led them to say, "Oh, did you finish your renovations? Could we see what you've done?"

I told them that I had neglected the house the last few weeks due to my book deadline and that I would feel much better if they would get the tour another time when I felt more prepared. But of course, they didn't care about my mess, and continued to share their enthusiasm for seeing the house anyway. I took a deep breath and asked myself, "What would keep me from showing them the house right now?" I heard a voice of truth inside of me say, "your pride."

Knowing that part of my growth has to do with learning to let go of guilt and shame when I can't attend to others' needs and to all of my responsibilities exactly when and how I'd like to, I further explored my feelings about their request. I asked myself, "What would be the best decision for my growth-to set a boundary and say, 'No, I really want you to come by later,' or to humble myself and let them connect with me in my messy world?" Asking this question, I instantly knew that perfectionism was the bigger block I needed to overcome, so I told them I'd give them a home tour. Their graciousness as they saw my home and my messiness offered me another layer of healing, helping me to realize that I could feel complete, even when life is a bit out of control.

When we slow down and choose what is most important to us, honoring our own growth, we can become clear about how to spend our time. Being in the flow of our clarity can save us time in the long run, as we are not wasting time on things that really aren't a priority to us, allowing ourselves to be driven by guilt and "shoulds."

Create a Time Journal and log your time. Slow down and take notice of how you are spending your time. Ask yourself: "What is most important to me? Is that what I am devoting the most time to?"

YOU CAN GET CLEAR BY ALLOWING YOUR EYES, EARS, AND GUT TO HEAR FOR YOU.

Often, we mistakenly believe that getting clear requires a lot of time. When I talk to my business clients about this concept, they envision taking a business retreat for several days to do some strategic planning or they think of the meetings they have attended in the past that have dragged on and on, so they resist the idea of taking time to get clear. In my personal life coaching, my clients often believe that they have to schedule time into their busy personal calendar if they want to get clear. They ask me if they should block out 30 minutes in the morning for meditation and 30 minutes in the evening for journaling. I tell them that while there is nothing wrong with doing these activities, they might be better served by making a habit of creating 60-second blocks of time throughout the day to become clear. This habit can keep us from getting so confused and cut off from our deepest values, feelings, and needs that we have to schedule large blocks of reflective time into our calendar just to find ourselves again.

You can become clear in a moment if you practice the 60-Second S.T.O.P. Technique. This technique will help you detach from what might be an emotionally intense situation so that you can receive guidance on what to do or say in a given situation that will lead to your feeling complete and not regretful. I developed the tool of the 60-Second S.T.O.P. Technique after learning that we often experience what brain researchers refer to as "the Beta state," an anxious state we live in when we are busy going about our lives and hardly breathing. This causes the corpus collosum, a structure in the brain that connects the left and right hemisphere, to contract. The result is less brainpower and less communication between the two hemispheres, especially when under stress.

On the other hand, when we slow down and breathe, and tune in to our anxiety, we are able to change our emotional response to a situation. We do this by detaching from our perceived crisis and seeing it as a catalyst to a new possibility. By perceiving the possibilities and asking ourselves, "How might I respond in a way that gets me what I ultimately want?" we're able to clearly recognize what would otherwise be our blind spot.

THE 60-SECOND S.T.O.P. TECHNIQUE WORKS LIKE THIS:

"S" – Slow down and breathe.

"T" – Tune in within. Ask yourself, "What am I feeling?" Connect with the emotional energy within you. Just notice it, without judging what you are feeling.

"O" – Observe what is happening around you. Get clear by connecting with the facts of what is happening-just notice, without judgment. Say to yourself, "Hmm . . . isn't that interesting? (Blank) is happening. Okay, it is what is what it is . . . "

"P" – Perceive the possibilities. Begin to wonder and get clear. Ask yourself, "Hmm . . . I wonder, what is my best possibility here for choosing what it is I want now, and in the long run?"

Stay open and curious and clarity will come to you. If you don't get an answer right away, do not get discouraged. You are building one of your personal leadership muscles, the inner muscle of consciousness that will help you to get clear. As with all things, growth takes time. The more you practice this technique, the easier it will be to get the answer to come to you in 60 seconds. Start to practice this technique when you are faced with the smaller crises in life so that when situations that would normally trigger fear and self-doubt come along, you'll be able to transmute your feelings more quickly and use the 60-Second S.T.O.P. Technique more effectively.

Practice the 60-Second S.T.O.P. Technique, which trains us to use our eyes, ears, and gut to become more clear.

LETTING GO OF PAST EXPERIENCES THAT ARE KEEPING YOU STUCK AND UNSURE OF HOW TO MOVE FORWARD WILL ALLOW YOU TO BECOME MORE CLEAR.

A contractor that was working out at my home for several days began to share with me a little bit about his life. He talked about how he was a Christian and had been disappointed in himself, others, and God because of his life's circumstances. At one time, he had been a multimillionaire and could have retired if it had not been for a bad market that caused him to lose a lot of money.

He also shared that he had been divorced and lost quite a bit of money in the divorce and not only suffered a financial setback but an emotional one as well. Although he didn't say it, I could tell that he was a bit frustrated and disappointed in God, since he felt that he had kept a promise to be pure if God would only send him the right woman. When he met his wife, she seemed perfect: She was beautiful, she was a Christian like he was, she seemed to like a lot of the same things he did, and she adored everything about him. "What else could I ask for?" he said.

When I thought about his question, I thought about how often we get impressed by images, instead of taking the time to get clear about who someone really is deep inside. When I asked him further about the relationship, he revealed that they married after knowing each other for only four months, and that there were signs prior to their marriage that she was abusing alcohol and experiencing strong mood swings.. He further explained that he ignored these problems because, despite his promise to God that he would remain celibate until he married, he became physically involved with her. It appeared as though his decision to marry her was made more out of guilt than clarity.

When I asked him how his life has been since his divorce, he continued to recite his list of disappointments. He talked about several medical conditions he'd suffered from and about a relationship he was currently in that was not working out.

When I asked him what he thought these experiences were trying to teach him, he suddenly got busy and began working on another part of the house. I didn't take it personally. I simply observed that what he was really walking away from was his past, and the lessons he would have to face if he were to move forward and become clear about how to live his life differently.

Many of us will spend years in a cycle of wanting to be someone's hero and then, when we don't feel that we are a hero, we will perceive ourselves as a victim. As a result, we will spend years persecuting someone else and blaming our unhappiness on them and our circumstances. In this way, we can continue to absolve ourselves from responsibility for the choices we've made and avoid learning the lessons of our past. When we hold on to disappointments, anger, and guilt, we stifle our ability to get clear about how to do things differently in our future.

To let go of past experiences that are keeping you stuck and unclear about how to move forward, practice the following steps:

Step 1: Recognize the person or people you need to let go of and forgive. Include God and yourself, if necessary.

Step 2: Recognize your state of mind and feelings.

Step 3: Let your feelings out. Tell God, write about your emotions in a journal, tell a friend, scream out loud, etc.

Step 4: Recognize the effect your feelings have had on your life. What consequences are you currently experiencing by holding on to the past?

Step 5: Now, ask to receive truth. Ask your Divine Source to help you to understand the lesson you are meant to learn.

Step 6: Make a commitment to be humble enough to hear the truth. Be open to admitting that you had a part to play in the unfolding of that situation.

Step 7: Ask your Divine Source to help you release any negative feelings you are still carrying about the person, the situation, or yourself, including feelings of sadness, hurt, fear, guilt, and anger.

Step 8: Choose a new way of looking at the situation. See it as an opportunity for your growth.

Step 9: Choose a new way to be in similar situations in the future, whether that means changing your perception of things, what you tell yourself about a situation, or what you choose in a similar situation.

Step 10: Choose a new behavior in the future. Be loving and honest with yourself as you choose new thoughts and behaviors, informed by the lessons you have learned.

> *If you are holding on to anger, sadness, or frustration about situations in your past and it's preventing you from moving forward, get clear about what you were supposed to learn from those experiences. This self-knowledge will set you free.*

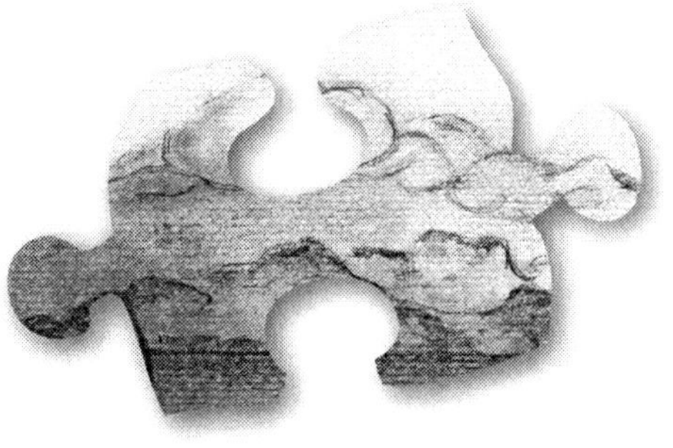

THIRD PIECE:

GET CALM! FIND THE PEACE IN THE STORM

Becoming calm is a necessary piece in the personal leadership puzzle because as we become calm, we let go of disturbing thoughts that lead to feelings, such as anxiety and depression, that inhibit our ability to feel complete, even in the best of circumstances and relationships. When we let go of disturbing thoughts and feelings, we create a stillness that gives us access to our inner guidance, which assists us and helps us to feel complete. Getting calm comes from a belief that life always works out for our best, if we just show up and participate with our heart wide open.

We're able to get calm when we trust in something bigger than our current situation and us. With this viewpoint, we can remain undisturbed even when we are in the most difficult situations, with the most difficult people. Putting together the pieces of curiosity, a clear mind, and a calm state of being, we can feel complete at work and at home.

OUR TEMPTATION IS TO GO INTO A FIGHT-OR-FLIGHT PATTERN OF SURVIVAL INSTEAD OF CHOOSING TO FIND THE PEACE IN THE STORM.

Why don't we practice getting calm on a regular basis, whenever we are dealing with difficulty? Often, it's because we allow ourselves to immediately go into a fight-or-flight response. This is a primitive, physical response to perceived danger. Our bodies tense up, adrenaline starts to pump through our veins, and we feel the need to fight someone or something, or flee as quickly as we can. Some of my clients prefer to call the fight response the "fix-it" response, because the action they often take when they're in this mode is to rush in and try to fix a situation or a person. Some have dubbed the flight response the "procrastination" response, because they often flee the danger by refusing to make a decision or deal with the situation at hand. I view the fight-or-flight response as being in a state of mind that causes us to want to avoid or control a situation, because we are not calmly viewing it from a possibility mindset. In any case, many things can throw us into what feels like a storm and trigger a fight-or-flight response, including:

1) Someone else's anger.
2) Someone else's cutting, blaming, and shaming remarks.
3) Someone else withholding warmth, love, affection, information, or support from us.
4) Our own fear, or sense of loss or shame.
5) Our own habits (such as how we deal with problems).
6) A feeling of being powerless, anxious, and overwhelmed.

7) The perception that we are in danger of some sort.

Whatever the triggers for our fight-or-flight response that keep us from getting calm in a storm, it's important to be aware that the thoughts and perceptions that agitate us are ones we can have control over. Although it may often feel as if something outside of us is causing us to feel upset and stressed out, it's not the dog running away, a flat tire, forgetting important papers we needed for a meeting, a breakup, or losing a big account that is causing us to react. And it's not something inside of us-the way we are wired, or our feelings of powerlessness, anxiousness, fear, or shame-that's to blame, either. The truth is that when we look at our situation from a perspective of personal leadership, we realize we are the power of our thoughts and therefore, we have the choice to remain calm as we deal with difficult situations.

Both the fight reaction and the flight reaction are normal responses, but they aren't the only responses we can have. Personal leadership allows us to make choices that offer us a complete life. We can choose to be proactive and be motivated by our values and goals instead of our fears. We can choose to find our peace in the storm, remaining calm as we notice the world around and within us, knowing that by getting calm, we are embracing an important missing piece in the leadership puzzle.

When I want to create calm amidst the storm, I will often ask myself, "What would 007 do right now?" After watching several of Pierce Bronson's James Bond movies, and having had the chance to meet him in person in Kauai once, I noticed that whether on camera or in real life, Pierce (007) knows how to keep cool, calm, and collected amidst the storm. I applied what I thought would be his technique one morning a while back, when I was getting ready to attend the Chicago Book Expo and got into a dangerous situation. My daughter and I were finishing up the final packing of the car, bringing books, displays, and information to distribute to the thousands of booksellers, publishers, and media representatives who would be there, and just as we were about to pull out of the driveway, I remembered that we had forgotten the brochure holders that were stored in the attic.

I drove back up the driveway and asked my daughter to assist me in getting the brochure holders down out of the attic space that was above the garage, reachable only by a four-by-four access panel and a tall ladder. I was already dressed for the expo, with my white shirt, black skirt, and high heels, so I asked my daughter if she would climb up the ladder and find the holders. As I held the ladder from below, I could hear her shouting to me, "Mom, I can't find them. Where are they?"

Of course, I knew that I could not go into the dusty old attic without getting dirty, so I thought, "If only I could climb up the ladder a few steps and peek into the attic, I could surely give her directions as to which box to look in." So I climbed up the ladder, grabbed the side of the attic opening, and begin to stick my head into the dusty old space to assist her. Just as we found the brochure holders and I was stepping down, my high heel got caught on the next step of the ladder, causing it to fall. There I was, hanging on to the ledge of the attic opening, 11 feet off the ground, with no ladder to support me.

My daughter, seeing me suddenly slip, began to scream, "Oh my gosh, Mom, are you okay?" Calmly, I took a deep breath and thought, "What would 007 do?" It may sound silly, but calmness came over me as I pictured James Bond dangling from a helicopter or a ledge, in a far more dangerous and difficult situation than I was in. Holding on and quickly accessing my curiosity, I assessed my options and chose the most viable one. I fixed my eyes on a landing point on the floor and decided I was going to jump. My daughter was screaming, frightened that I was going to get hurt, and I calmly said, "Lisa, you can help me best by breathing deeply with me, okay?" So she did. When I felt ready, I let go and landed on the balls of my feet, slightly forward so that I could brace myself with my hands and keep myself from falling onto my back and potentially hurting myself. I stood up and realized I had done it: I'd found a safe way to get out of the dangerous situation I'd been in. Lisa and I were deeply relieved.

For me, imagining myself as cool and collected as James Bond is a great way to switch into a feeling of calmness. Taking a deep breath, as Lisa did, is another way to slow down the panicky thoughts in your head so that you can get calm. When you find the calm amidst the storm, you may be surprised at the clever solutions you come up with that take you out of stressful and even dangerous situations.

When you find yourself in a difficult situation, take a deep breath. Find your state of calm by asking yourself, "How might I deal with this difficult situation?" or ask, "What would 007 do?"

AS WE GO ABOUT BUILDING A COMPLETE LIFE, WE MAY MISTAKENLY BELIEVE WE HAVE TO BE STRESSED OUT IN ORDER TO REACH OUR DESTINATION, WHEN REALLY, WE NEED TO GET CALM.

We cause ourselves stress when we think it is vitally important to achieve a certain goal and convince ourselves that we will not be able to achieve it, or even if we do, we won't be able to sustain our success. Unfortunately, lurking inside many of us is a deep belief that we are not "enough" regardless of what we have on the outside. We might believe that we are not:

worthy enough

competent enough

lovable enough

loving enough

smart enough

good-looking enough

fit enough

strong enough

soft enough

or

talented enough

(The list goes on and on.)

We begin to experience emotional and physical stress when we apply force to a situation, trying hard to make something happen instead of just showing up and being our best self, trusting and allowing others to do the same. When we try to force our life to be a particular way or we try to force a particular outcome, we lose our composure and believe it is the situation that's causing us to be stressed. When we come from a personal leadership point of view, we can see that it is within our reach to grab the third piece of the personal leadership puzzle and get calm!

In a recent business coaching session, I shared this example with a client who was stressed out about several situations at work, including interactions he was having with co-workers and a lower monthly revenue, which he feared would keep him from meeting his year-end sales goal. After he spent about 20 minutes sharing with me his list of outside stressors, I said, "Imagine that there are two households next to one another. Both households have the exact same situations: They both have young parents, three young children, bills to pay, and just about the same amount of income. The difference is that in one household, the parents meet together on a regular basis, when the kids are asleep. They are aware of the situations before them, they make a point of talking about their feelings including their fears and feelings of inadequacy, and then, together, they strategize to solve their problems and make their decisions. The parents in the other household, however, tend to handle things differently. They notice a situation and panic because they think they are not 'enough' to handle it. They don't share their feelings with one another, but instead switch off from bickering to blaming to blackmailing the other, vowing that they will leave if things don't change."

After presenting to him these two scenarios, I asked, "Which one do you think would have a better chance at success, household number one or household number two?"

He chose household number one. When I asked him why, he said, "First of all, household number one approaches things openly, and with curiosity about each other's point of view and feelings. They also approach things with a sense of calm as they problem solve together. The other household is so full of stress that they can't connect at any level."

"Precisely," I told him. "Now, let's bring that back to you and your situation. How would this be similar to how you approach things at work? I think we agree that 'stuff happens,' right? Can you see how your approach to your own fears and self-doubts, when shared open and calmly, can help others to open up and calmly approach situations too?"

"Boy," he said, "opening up my fears to my wife about our kids and finances is one thing, but to my employees . . . that's a whole other topic!"

I asked him with curiosity and a sense of calm, "Why is that situation different?"

"Well," he thought, "you aren't supposed to share your emotions at work."

"Who said?" I inquired.

"I'm not sure, but it's understood that that's the way it is in business."

"Okay," I said, "but maybe there is a way we could look at that differently. Consider this. There is a huge elephant in the room. Everyone knows that someone just got fired. They also know that your company just lost its biggest account. In addition, it is obvious that you've cut back on spending, because you just sent out a memo saying so. Now maybe you haven't added up all these pieces of the equation for them, but most people who are even partially intuitive would get a sense that something has changed, wouldn't you agree?"

He nodded.

"Okay then," I went on to say, "now imagine that you have three ways to deal with this: First, you could pretend life is good and just bounce into work acting as if all is fine, denying to yourself and others that there is an issue, in order to save face and avoid any negative reaction from them. Secondly, you could go to them and start crying on their shoulder and tell them you are a victim of circumstances, or get angry and blame them for the situation, spewing all of your raw emotion on to them. Or, third, you could admit that things have changed, share your concern for the future, and invite them to strategize and work together with you as a team to make the necessary adjustments to get on the path toward victory."

I waited to see what he was thinking. After giving him a little space, I said, "So what do you think . . . if you were in my job, which option would you recommend to your client?"

The answer seemed so obvious to him, I could tell he was a bit embarrassed and perhaps annoyed. I was getting him to look at something from a detached point of view, whereas in the past, he was used to fretting about it, allowing his unexplored, turbulent emotions to skew his perspective.

Instead of answering my question, he asked one in return: "Well, what if I tell the truth, and one of my employees gets scared and looks for another job?"

I let him sit in his fear for a minute, and then calmly answered him. "That's a definite possibility. But my question is this: And if they do, so what?"

"So what! So . . . I need them to do their job. It's a tough market out there. It's hard to find people for that position at that salary."

Once again, I just noticed his fear and self-doubt and calmly observed it with curiosity, clarity, and a sense of calm. I wondered, "Why doesn't he feel the market is 'enough,' that his business is 'enough' to attract an employee and offer a competitive salary? Why doesn't he feel that he is 'enough' to keep a good employee?"

Wondering this, I sat for a moment in silence.

Finally, he spoke. "Well, if they go, they probably weren't committed or much of a team player anyway, right?"

"Precisely," I said. "So then, why operate out of fear, judgment, and a need to be in control? Why be stressed out most of the time, when you could be more open and trusting, and allow life to unfold as it needs to?"

"Wow! Now, that's a stretch!' he said. "It's hard for me to trust my employees to hang in there when times are tight. I guess deep down I believe that if it's meant to be, it's up to me."

"You think you're really powerful, don't you?" I asked.

"At times," he admitted. "But sometimes, it feels just the opposite."

"I thought so. You see, the opposite of pride is shame. If you are the center of your own universe, then when things go right, you think it was all because of you. When things go wrong, you think it was all because of you, too. You hold yourself responsible for everything. That's a very stressful way to live, don't you think?"

Again, I paused so he had a chance to reflect on my question.

"I never thought of it that way," he said.

Instead of working yourself into a state of anxiety and fear over a difficult situation, you can choose to create a sense of calm within the storm, and in that calm, allow yourself to be trusting and open. In this way, you will open yourself up to receive the assistance of others instead of feeling that you have to solve all your problems by yourself.

Stay calm as you move toward your destination, dealing calmly with the daily stuff along the way.

OUTER DIFFICULT CIRCUMSTANCES ARE
NOTHING MORE THAN A MIRROR REFLECTION
OF THE TURMOIL WE ARE HOLDING WITHIN.

As we discover the benefits of slowing down, we find our inner sanctuary. We enter the doorway to getting calm when we allow ourselves to become curious and we clear our mind instead of focusing on the difficulty of the circumstances before us. Creating a sense of curiosity and getting clear quiets the judgmental mind and brings us back into our heart and spirit.

But of course, life brings us surprises that can feel like storms and that test our ability to stay in our calm state of mind. These storms can come in varying forms. Depending on our preferences, values, prior awareness, and feelings in the situation, news can either hit us as a confirmation of what we already knew and thus be a relief, or it can blindside us and throw us off balance. In many cases, it is not the situation itself that causes the storm, but what we say to ourselves about the situation and the added "story" we create around the facts of the situation. For example:

- You may discover that your child was caught smoking. You could create a bigger storm for yourself by telling yourself that your child is on a slippery slope and that you are to blame for not being a more attentive parent.

- You may learn that your spouse had an affair. You may create a bigger storm for yourself by telling yourself that no one is to be trusted.

- You may realize that your bank account is overdrawn. You may create a bigger storm for yourself by telling yourself that you are totally irresponsible and can never do things right.

- You might have just found out you were fired. You may create a bigger storm for yourself by telling yourself that the job market out there is so bad that you will never find a job.

- You might have just lost a client. You make a bigger storm for yourself by telling yourself that you will never make your quota and will have a hard time paying your bills this month.

- Someone you love may have just died. You may create a bigger storm for yourself by telling yourself that life will never be as much fun.

- You may have just been diagnosed with cancer. You create a bigger storm for yourself by telling yourself that you know you are going to die.

Difficult situations can lead us into the storm and trigger deprivation thinking: We start telling ourselves that we are not "enough" and that our circumstances are not "enough." This can leave us feeling very powerless, anxious, and alone.

To get calm in the storm, you must find your curiosity and get clear. You can do this by asking yourself these two questions:

1. *"Hmm . . . isn't that interesting?* I wonder how I am feeling about this?" This question will help you get curious and clear about emotions you are experiencing, helping you

reconnect with yourself and taking your focus off of the troubling situation so that you can become calm.

Now, you might think, "What kind of crazy question is that? That won't lead me to getting calm! It will only lead me to hurt, sadness, anxiety, frustration, and powerlessness!" Perhaps at first you might have to deal with these feelings, but remember: The only way out of the storm is through the door of curiosity. If you discover these more uncomfortable feelings with the first question, go deeper into curiosity and clarity and soon you will get calm.

2. ***"What am I to learn?"*** This question will lead you to let go of the past and walk through the doorway of new possibilities. New possibilities cannot even be entertained until you have first connected with your whole self. By connecting with your whole self, you are able to feel the energy that is flowing in your body, including the energy of your emotions. After all, emotions are pure energy. It just so happens that we put negative labels on certain types of emotional energy. For instance, we think that sadness, powerlessness, hurt, fear, and frustration are negative emotions. Yet, there is no such thing as negative emotions, just uncomfortable ones.

You can also look at emotions like jealousy and pride as sinful, yet if you approach these emotions with curiosity versus judgment, you can explore what is behind them. When you do that openly, you can become clear about what they are trying to tell you. You will get calm as you integrate with your emotions and allow them to flow in your body.

When you can look at all of your emotions as forms of energy that want to help you propel yourself forward, you can connect with your energy and move it through your body. This will cause a more balanced brain state, often referred to as "brain synchronicity." This balanced condition has been noted by researchers who have done EEG studies and it is the state that expert meditators put themselves in regularly. Dr. Lester Fehmi, director of the Biofeedback Research Center at Princeton University, has said that brain synchronization "represents the maximum efficiency of information transport through the brain . . . you feel more aware . . . and function more intuitively." (from the article "Science Behind the Holosync"). Brain synchronization allows us to be more creative, innovative, and intuitive, and to be better at solving problems. And research has found that getting calm through relaxation, systematically relaxing all muscles while repeating a personally meaningful focus word or phrase, can help people to solve problems in difficult situations.

Allowing your emotions to move through you will help you get calm as you consider the new possibilities before you and ask yourself the very curious and clear question, "What do I need to learn?"

Deal with the turmoil within before you try to address the outer turmoil, by practicing the habit of brain synchronicity.

CLEARING OUT THE EMOTIONAL MUCK HELPS US TO GET CALM AGAIN.

When we avoid labeling our feelings as good or bad, right or wrong, and instead just feel them and move through them, we stop getting stuck in the emotional muck. Years of avoiding the questions "What do I feel?" and "What do I need to learn?" can cause us to accumulate a lot of unattended-to emotional muck. To move through your feelings, notice them without judgment. Open yourself up to learning from them, knowing that they will pass with time-it may take a few seconds, a few minutes, or a few hours, but they will pass.

When we don't notice our emotions and move through them, we gather emotional muck. Emotional muck is the dense energy within us that remains after a perceived storm in our life. When we do not deal with feelings from a storm and do not clean up afterward by asking ourselves, "What do I feel?" and "What do I need to learn?" we are left with a lot of emotional muck. The emotional muck is attached to beliefs we hold about ourselves after years of what we call "bad experiences." These beliefs are lies we tell ourselves, and they can include the following:

- *Life is hard.*
- *I never get a break.*
- *I just can't handle crises.*
- *No one else has it this hard.*
- *God must not care about me.*
- *I must be too sensitive and too emotional.*

(The list goes on and on)

Like most people, I started to accumulate emotional muck in my early childhood. I was the intuitive one in the family, sensing the family dynamics and secrets regarding my birth father. When I would speak my truth about this situation, I would get comments back like, "Where did you get that silly imagination from?" Instead of realizing that these comments were a way to stop the conversation, I took the criticism and scolding personally and believed that something must be wrong with me. I told myself that I was too sensitive, too difficult, and too much for anyone to handle and love.

Of course, as most of us do, later in life, I chose relationships with people who matched up with my issues. The men I got involved with had a familiar way of avoiding difficult conversations. We choose to be around people who confirm our beliefs about ourselves that we've held since childhood, whether or not those people are good for us. These choices not only keep us in our comfort zone initially, but they also put us in situations that bring up our emotional muck so that we can deal with it, heal it, and release it. Usually, we begin to clean out the emotional muck when we decide to get curious, clear, and calm enough to look at the truth behind the muck.

Our emotional muck is created when we begin to wonder:

- Is something wrong with me?
- Am I "enough"?
- Is God "enough"?

Asking these types of questions leads us to begin to doubt ourselves and, as a result, we begin to lose our sense of personal power, because we have lost our awareness of who we are and what we want.

I remember one client in particular who dared to go clean up his emotional muck. We had been working together for some time, and the cognitive skills I was teaching him and his employees in training and coaching were not making a difference in a particular work situation with an employee he often interacted with. He was the owner of a small company and was having issues with this particular manager who would tend to keep information from him, dismiss his requests, and not include him in decision making. It was my client's impression that this employee was probably dominating the other people in his department, using force to get others to perform exactly the way he wanted them to and just doing the task himself if they didn't do it his way. When I asked my client, "Why do you keep him on?" he said, "Because thanks to him, our sales have doubled in the last four years."

It was clear that my client had an either/or attitude: I either accept this behavior or I let him go. This limited thinking causes us to feel powerless and anxious, and that creates emotional muck inside of us.

After listening to my client and trying more standard approaches of teaching direct communication, which didn't work with him, I decided it was time to clear out the emotional muck that had built up for years.

We began to breathe deeply and slowly and went for the clean up. With his permission, I took my client through a body scan, relaxing him with breath and visualization from head to toe. We began by imagining a white light coming through the top of his head and entering his body, like a billowy cloud. We moved this white light through his entire head, softening the tension in his eyes, cheeks, jaw, and throat with more visualization and slow, deep breathing. Then I had him breathe more deeply into his body, opening up his chest and the tension he held. Softening his shoulders, he continued deep breathing as we created an image of white light erasing any darkness that was being held in his arms. I asked him to expand his body by breathing through his fingertips, opening himself up to the life support of his breath. We took the white light again through his heart, down into the more dense area of his stomach.

Next, I asked him to feel the density in his body, the dark emotion that he stored in his stomach. I asked him to identify this emotion, and he said that it was fear. Then I asked him to reflect on this question, "What is this emotion trying to tell me about my situation with this employee?"

We paused for a moment so he could listen to the wisdom of his body as he became calm and curious, and his body provided him with clarity. He said, "I'm afraid that if I tell him he can't treat me and others with disregard and dominance that he'll quit, or stay and stop trying to make a profit for the company. Anything I do, I am stuck."

I asked him to imagine his worst thought coming true. I watched him tense up, and after I knew that he was finished visualizing this scenario, I asked him to focus on the feeling in his stomach again and ask himself, "What am I now feeling?" His answer was, "Alone, afraid, and powerless."

This signaled to me that it was time to go clean up the emotional muck, the gunk that holds our unconscious, negative beliefs about ourselves, such as the belief that we are not enough to handle situations we perceive to be difficult.

I invited him to explore his emotional muck more deeply. "Are you ready to stop feeling powerless and anxious and instead feel strong enough to handle any response he might choose?" I asked.

His answer was "Yes."

"Okay then, let's go do some house cleaning."

I asked him to continue breathing deeply and slowly and said, "Imagine that white light again. Now feel it going deep into your hip and pelvis area. What does this area feel like and look like?"

After a few moments, he answered, "Dark and dense and totally black."

I invited him to go into the dark, dense, black area with his breath and the white light, feeling the power of his breath and light and noticing how he could clear out the density with his mind. I asked him to get curious, clear, and calm and to ask himself these questions, one at a time:

"What is this density trying to tell me?"

"What old beliefs am I telling myself about myself, beliefs that I accumulated over the years because of difficult and disappointing situations?"

After about a minute, he said, "I am not adequate by myself."

As he said this, I could hear and feel his sadness tightening his throat. I knew his history and intuitively sensed where this false belief came from. His was a family business that he had inherited from his father. Although he was the owner now, he was still perceiving himself like a little boy, dependent on his father to tell him what to do in the business. He had never gone off on his own to find his true self and his own power. I knew we were visiting the emotional muck so that he could clear it out and regain his own personal leadership.

I encouraged him to feel his emotions and transform into the leader he wanted to be. I said, "Clear out the old emotional muck. Feel, cough, cry, howl-whatever you need to do to let it go. Let go of your old beliefs about yourself not being 'enough,' so that you can make room for your greatness."

He started to cough, loosening the phlegm in his throat, and sniffling to clear of his sinuses.

I reminded him, "Don't hold the energy. Let it out so you can transform from feeling inadequate to feeling empowered in your own personal leadership. Your feelings are simply energy. Don't judge them or yourself. You need to feel them in order to transform. Cough, blow your nose, cry-whatever is there, let it flow."

Then, as I could tell he was done clearing himself of his false belief and his fear, I helped him do the final cleansing of his emotional muck. I asked him to imagine the white light and breathe slowly and deeply again, so that he could clean up the details.

"Feel who you are right now. Feel the power in your body. You are 'enough' for any situation. Now, with your power of knowing who you really are, clean up any residual emotional muck. Go deeper. Take your breath and the light and go deep down into the base of your body. With your breath, go down your legs and connect your feet to the ground. Notice how your feet are full of energy and so is your body. Feel how your feet connect to the energy of the ground. Notice how the ground is supporting your feet. Now breathe through your body and feel how big and full you are. . . . I want you to go back in your mind's eye and imagine yourself noticing that this manager has stopped trying because you confronted him about his behavior. Tell me, how do you know he's stopped trying? What is he doing? What is he saying? How is he acting?"

I paused for a moment to ensure that my client was listening to his inner wisdom in a curious, clear, and calm way. When I knew he was hearing himself, I continued.

"Notice your employee's choice. Remain curious, clear, and calm. Say to yourself, 'Hmm . . . isn't that interesting? He has stopped trying since I confronted him.' Now connect with your inner wisdom and ask yourself, 'What am I feeling?'"

He answered, "Angry."

"Good. Anger is an emotion that tells us that something needs to change. Now ask your inner wisdom, 'What is it I need to learn so that I can make a change?'"

His answer was, "To confront him about his lack of enthusiasm when he can't be the one in control."

"Great. Now with your breath expanding throughout your

whole body, watch yourself confronting him calmly and clearly. What are you saying to him?"

He answered as though he was talking right to his employee, saying, "I have noticed that since our conversation about your management style that you have gone to the other extreme in your behavior. Instead of being at the office and acting angry and in control most of the time, now you are acting unenthusiastic and passive. That's not the change I was requesting. What I need from you is for you to be an effective leader in this organization, and that means you have to step up and engage with others. I need you to notice their behavior, as I am doing with you right now, and help them get past where they are stuck and help them to be their best self. Instead of feeling powerless to help them, and then taking over or writing them off, I need you to have a conversation with them to help them grow. How might you do that?"

I could see that we had helped my client clear out his own emotional muck. He was now sensing his own personal leadership and thus could help others find theirs.

As I say in my training courses, "The speed of the leader is the speed of the gang." When we clean out our own emotional muck, we can help others clean out theirs.

Emotional muck can accumulate in our personal life as well. Some people might consider this to be like "baggage," but I think of it differently. When someone has slowed down enough in his life to get clear, feel what he needs to feel, learn from it, and move on to make better choices, I believe he is without emotional muck. Baggage, on the other hand, might be the consequence of our choices from the past. For example, perhaps your impulsive spending caused you to go into bankruptcy. You may have learned what you needed from that situation, but are still working out of your consequences of debt-you are still dealing with your baggage. Personally, I would much rather deal with someone who has baggage than with someone who has emotional muck. Emotional muck keeps us stuck. Baggage builds our strength, as it reminds us of the consequences of our bad choices, thus sharpening our discernment.

Get calm in the midst of a storm by detaching from your difficult circumstances and focusing on your emotions and what they are trying to tell you.

WE CAN BECOME CALM BY ASKING OURSELVES ONE QUESTION AT A TIME.

When you are anxious, you can begin to get calm by asking yourself certain questions. For example, below is a list of situations you might be unclear and anxious about and the questions you could ask yourself. When you ask these questions, be sure that you are curious, clear, and calm. Do not judge the answer that comes up, or the feelings you experience. Simply listen to your inner wisdom as you explore your answers.

- You are unclear and anxious about a relationship you are in. You wonder if the other person is interested in you. You can ask yourself, "I wonder if this person truly is interested in me?"

- You are confused and anxious about a relationship and wonder if you are interested in someone. You can ask yourself, "I wonder, am I truly interested in this person?"

- You are unsure and anxious about whether or not you want to take a particular job. You can ask yourself, "I wonder, what is causing my ambiguity and anxiety about this particular job?"

- You are unsure and anxious about where you want to go on vacation. You can ask yourself, "I wonder, where do I truly want to go on vacation?"

When we dialog with ourselves and ask ourselves one question at a time, we become calm as we discover what we need to do or say in a particular situation. Instead of asking ourselves one good question at a time, we often just say to ourselves and others, "I don't know . . . I'm confused." This thought does not help us to get curious and clear and to calmly approach the issue. Instead, it just keeps us feeling stuck.

If we ask ourselves questions about a particular person or situation, often, we bombard ourselves with too many questions all at once. When we are asking ourselves many questions at a time, with hardly a breath in between, we create chaos instead of becoming calm. Chaotic questioning is a string of questions put together such that our subconscious mind cannot register our request for clarity and calm. It might sound something like, "I wonder, should I take this job or the other one?" quickly followed by, "Will this job have advancement opportunities?" and "Will I enjoy the people I work with?"

When you are feeling so anxious that you cannot settle yourself down and ask just one question at a time, you can benefit from using the One-Minute Meditation you learned about earlier. Following is how you might use it in this particular circumstance.

THE ONE-MINUTE MEDITATION FOR QUIETING AN ANXIOUS STRING OF THOUGHTS

1. *Detach from the person or situation in your life that is troubling you.* Do this by saying to yourself, "Hmm . . . isn't that interesting? I wonder, what is troubling me?" This puts you in a neutral, observant, nonjudgmental, and curious state of mind. Simply be curious at first.

2. *Connect with your inner wisdom.* Ask yourself, "What question do I need to ask myself to get clear in this situation?" A friend who has her own Christian

counseling center told me that she asks her clients to ask themselves, "If I had one question I could ask God in order to get clear right now, what would it be?"

3. ***Be still and listen.*** Breathe in deeply and as you do, say to yourself, "I breathe in peace." Now exhale deeply, saying, "I breathe out anxiety and fear." Do this several times. This exercise helps you to open up your heart so you can get out of your "chatterbox" head and become clear about what it is you have been wondering about.

4. ***Do "squared" breathing.*** There are four steps to squared breathing, just as there are four sides to a square: Inhale for four counts. Hold for four counts. Exhale for four counts. Hold for four counts. Repeat.

Stay in this place of silence and place of calm for as long as you can. When you begin to think of the things you are anxious about, imagine yourself writing your concerns on a piece of paper and then setting it aside, knowing you will deal with it later.

Now come back to your state of stillness and place of calm. Ask yourself, "What question am I most wondering about that would help me to get clear about (blank)?"

Take mini-breaks throughout the day,
using a One-Minute Meditation.
It will help you to stay calm as you face challenges.

FOURTH PIECE:

GET CONFIDENT! FLY FREE FROM WORRY

Confidence, the fourth piece of the personal leadership puzzle, is the self-assuredness that comes from being connected to one's inner wisdom and true essence. When we have confidence, we operate from a positive belief system, and find ourselves saying "I can" and "It's possible." We are able to ask directly for what we need and do not feel embarrassed about being "bold" or "presumptuous," even in the face of another person's judgment. If someone is uncomfortable with our directness, we do not become defensive and start feeling guilty or ashamed.

When confident people strive to succeed, they ask themselves, "How might I succeed?" versus "Can I succeed?" They tend to trust in themselves, to believe that they can overcome adversity, so they are able to go after what they want and need without much hesitation. If they are fearful initially, they quickly overcome it. Because of their confident mindset, they are able to persevere, and to feel complete even when they haven't quite reached their goal or desired destination. This is because they have an inner knowing that tells them that they will achieve their dreams in perfect timing. Because they are void of the anxiety or depression that would tell them otherwise, they are able to accept where they are in the process of unfoldment without feeling scattered.

Confident people do not get attached to the form life takes; they go with the ebb and flow of life, seeing the possibilities before them, being resilient, and forging forward despite obstacles. They overcome their fear using their inner wisdom, and then overcome obstacles to their goals. This is why they are often able to achieve the results they desire.

WE OFTEN DON'T RECOGNIZE OUR FEAR

AS A TEMPORARY STATE OF BEING.

As we transform out of our fear and self-doubt, we realize that the illusions of safety, security, love, and belonging were there to trick us into believing that they could set us free and make us feel complete. Instead of living in this illusion that we can live our lives without having to face adversity, challenge, or unexpected change, we discover that the only way to be free is to transform out of our fear and find our confidence. Reclaiming our confidence, we can be who we truly are at our essence instead of living according to our fears of others' disapproval, of not being "enough," and so on. Then we are able to experience greater fulfillment and abundance in our lives, at work and at home, because we are flying free, letting go of our attachments to the illusions of safety, security, love, and belonging. We are able to live in the present moment, accepting what our circumstances are right now rather than grieving the losses of the past or wishing that something would change. We feel complete.

Confidence is not a static condition of always feeling sure of ourselves. It is a state of being that allows us to quickly transform from being fearful to connecting with our essence on a regular basis. Living in a state of confidence allows us to make moment-to-moment choices that honor ourselves and the highest good of the all.

Confidence is the result of doing inner work, identifying our fear, and committing to move through it. This allows us to choose what is right for us even when we are feeling pressure to betray our deepest feelings, beliefs, and goals.

Teenagers often feel pressured to betray who they are because they have a strong need to belong, and this can lead them into undesirable behaviors such as using alcohol or drugs or engaging in inappropriate and even dangerous sexual behaviors. The truth is that many of us are like teenagers in adult bodies-we are still abandoning our true essence to keep up with the Joneses, feel that we belong at work, and feel like we are someone special.

To complete the personal leadership puzzle, we need to do inner work, becoming aware of our fears about a lack of safety, security, love, and belonging, because these fears can lead us astray from making confident choices that honor who we really are at our essence. Instead of feeling ashamed for being different from others, we can feel proud and confident. When we can consciously name the fear we are feeling within, we can begin to observe our fear, bless it for wanting to protect us, and move on to fly free and make our dreams come true.

I was reminded of this recently when I came home from Chicago from an evening of celebration. I could hardly keep my eyes open on the drive home, but as I walked into my home at 2:30 A.M. and climbed up my three-story staircase, I was awakened by my cats, Mo and George, going crazy chasing a bird that was flying around inside my bedroom. It swooped up toward the vaulted ceiling, trying desperately to escape through the skylights or any window it could find. I couldn't believe my eyes. How did this bird get in the house? Too exhausted to deal with anything, I grabbed the cats, took them out of the bedroom, removed the sash from my belt loops, closed the swinging doors, and tied them shut. Not knowing what I could do to solve the problem, and too tired to figure it out, I simply prayed, "Lord, this one is for you to take care of." (And please make sure it doesn't poop all over my house!)

That night, I peacefully slept downstairs in my daughter Alex's bedroom, believing all would be just fine.

The next morning, I woke up and untied the door to my bedroom. In my wishful thinking, I'd half hoped that the bird would've just disappeared, but there it was. I was disappointed, but I practiced the first three pieces of the personal leadership puzzle: I got curious, clear, and calm. I asked God, "Okay, so you didn't take the bird away. What am I to do or learn from this?" What I heard was:

"Call the Humane Society Rescue Mission."

That's exactly what I did. A kind gentleman answered the phone and began to talk me through how to get this black, hook-beaked bird back to freedom. As I followed the gentleman's suggestion and covered the windows and opened the patio doors, so the bird could find the opening, I realized how nervous I was. Thank goodness he was on the phone, so he didn't realize I had just assembled a suburban combat outfit. It consisted of a large white Tupperware bowl placed on my head to protect it; a thick, white, terry cloth robe to keep my skin from being scratched, reading glasses to protect my eyes, and a broom just in case the bird should get scared enough to attack. If the armor itself wouldn't protect me, perhaps the sight of my outfit would be scary enough for the bird to stay away!

Although I had become fearful, I knew the goal was to transform from feeling fear to feeling confidence. I focused on the journey, not the destination, trusting that confidence would arrive, but hoping it would arrive quickly. Although the man on the phone could not see me, he must have sensed my hesitation and fear. He said, "Remember, the bird is more scared than you are." I laughed and said, "Don't be so sure!" His voice got calm and he said, "No, really, look at the bird's tail-I'll bet it's flipping up and down in fear right now." Indeed it was, and I could now see the vulnerability of the fearful bird that was trapped in my home.

As the man from the Humane Society helped me focus on becoming compassionate for the terrified bird, I suddenly transformed my own fear into courage and confidence. The three of us-the man, the bird, and I-were quietly aware of one another. I watched the bird's tail continue fluttering until slowly, he become a little less agitated. He looked over at me and we made deep eye contact and, within a minute, the bird's tail became nearly still. I was amazed at how the man on the phone's presence, so clear, calm, and confident, helped me to arrive at my own place of clarity, calm, and confidence and thus affected the bird's state. From my new place of strength and clarity, I was finally ready to assist the bird to fly free.

I walked over to the patio door and opened it, and a brisk winter breeze entered the bedroom. The bird walked over, past the patio doors, and missed his chance to escape. I gently pleaded with the bird, "Oh no, birdie! Back here! Fly free! Fly free!" It was as if he could hear me and understood what I was saying as he backed up and stood right in front of the open patio door once again. He looked at me and we stood once more, eyeing each other for what seemed to be at least a minute. I stood in curiosity: Why wouldn't he just fly out when he had a chance to be free?

Watching the bird as he stood there in hesitation, I was reminded of many experiences in my own life and the lives of those I coached and trained. I thought about how often we get ourselves into a place we don't want to be in, and when the door is clearly open for our release, we often are afraid to step out into the unknown. We let our fear overrule our desire for change.

At that moment, I knew why this bird was trapped in my house: He couldn't see his opportunity to freedom because his fear was blinding him to the open door in front of him. When we give in to fear, we, too, do not see the opportunities to freedom. This situation was meant to make me realize that I needed to write about transforming fear into confidence. And just as this idea came to me in great clarity, the bird suddenly unfolded his wings, headed out the door, and flapped his way to freedom.

Transform your fear and become confident by identifying your fear, exploring it in order to learn from it, and remembering that it is only a temporary feeling leading you back to your confidence.

WHEN WE TAKE THE CONSCIOUS ENERGY OF FEAR

AND TRANSFORM IT INTO CONFIDENCE,

WE SEE HOW POWERFUL WE ARE.

I couldn't be certain of how the bird got in the house that night. Of course, the first thing I checked was the fireplace to see if the chimney flue was open, and it was, so it was easy to conclude that the bird had gotten in through that route. But not even two months later, one morning at about 5:30, one of my cats started acting up again, meowing over and over again. In my drowsiness, I groggily yelled to Mo, "Be quiet! It's not time to get up yet!" I was certain he was up to his usual cat antics, wanting to play as soon as the sun came up through the two-story windows and skylight. His internal time clock has always been different from mine. After several attempts to hush him, I decided I had to get out of bed and see what was going on. I discovered he was in the loft area off my master bedroom, and sure enough, another bird that looked exactly like the first one was in the house.

The bird was sitting on the ledge of one of the windows, and it was obvious that he had aggressively tried to fly out of the closed windows, as he and the glass were both covered in blood. This time, I didn't grab the white Tupperware hat or the terry cloth robe for protection. Instead, I took myself to a place where I was clear, calm, and confident, and reminded myself that the bird was more scared than I was. Remembering what had worked before with the other bird, I remained in my stillness and stared him down. His fluttering tail calmed, just as the other bird's tail had calmed when I made eye contact. I opened the French doors off the loft and began to walk toward the bird, directing him toward the door. He let me get within two feet of him and didn't move. Because of the blood, I wondered whether he had hurt his wing and was unable to fly. I went into the bathroom to get a towel in case I needed to pick him up. As I approached him a second time, this time getting mere inches away, he exploded into flight and violently began to fight to find his way out, again smacking himself against the windows and the walls.

A moment of clarity came to me as I observed him. I thought about how these two birds had such different responses to their dilemma. The first chose to flee by avoiding taking action (in other words, he hesitated when he encountered the opportunity of the open door, perhaps because he wasn't confident and sure of himself). The other bird had chosen to fight, and he was fighting so hard to control his situation that he'd hurt himself. Again, I couldn't help but think about myself and others and how, like these birds, we often go about trying to find our way and reaching our destination by choosing to flee (perhaps procrastinating) or fight (perhaps by aggressively trying to "fix" matters without thinking clearly). I thought, "If only we could learn to be more discerning while moving more gracefully and connecting to our essence, we would be much more likely to get to where we want to go and to feel that our lives are complete."

Once again, as soon as I had an awareness of why I was having a strange encounter with a bird in my home, and had taken the time to reflect upon it, the bird took flight toward freedom, as if on cue.

I stood there shaking my head, saying, "Lord, what was this all about?" What I heard was:

"You are the power of your thoughts.

Your thoughts will set you free."

For days, I kept thinking about these incidents as I wondered how the birds had gotten in. I knew it couldn't have been through the chimney since I had closed the flue after the first incident. I asked anyone who was familiar with my house to venture a guess, but no one had any ideas.

One week later, I was rummaging around in one of my closets that I rarely use because it is full of clothes that are either outdated or I no longer fit into. As I thought about the clothes I no longer had any use for but was still hanging on to, I thought about how, when we are not confident of ourselves, we cling to things longer than we need to for one reason or another. I considered why I still had these clothes, and realized I was hanging on to them out of fear. Might I change my mind someday and want them? Something in me that made me realize it was time to do a major cleansing, letting go of the old, fearful thoughts and replacing them with confidence that something better was in store for me in the future.

As I had this awakening, I looked up and saw that a large access panel that leads to the attic had been moved out of place, exposing an opening to the attic. It's likely that the panel had been left that way after my building inspection nine months previous. I now knew that this is how the birds were coming in. I could imagine how the birds saw the light from the windows the few times I had opened up that closet door, and were attracted to it. The next day, I called my home repairman who found a small, unfinished area under the roofline of my house that had enabled the birds to get into the attic and eventually, into my house. It seems that the mystery of the birds was meant to help me see how I was allowing myself to keep hanging on to the old-old clothes, old beliefs, and old fears-and perhaps preventing myself from seeing opportunities that were right in front of me. This experience reminded me of how when we are leading our lives conscious of our thoughts, we are able to transform fear into confidence.

The incidents with the birds also helped me to remember that when we are confident, we have the ability to help others transform from confusion to clarity, anxiety to calm, and self-doubt to confidence. We are constantly sending people messages, whether directly, through our words, or indirectly, through our thoughts and presence. Confidence not only benefits us, it benefits those around us, because it allows us to help them transform their fear into confidence, too.

Nothing is more fulfilling than to be connected to your true essence, the part of you that is free from fear and embraced by love. In this place of freedom and complete presence, you will be more awake to receive inner guidance in the moment. This guidance will give you the confidence you need to move forward in your life and develop a sense of completeness.

Transform you fear into your confidence by recognizing that fear is only a temporary state of mind. Understanding this, you can help yourself and others to take advantage of opportunities that allow us to reconnect with our powerful presence.

CONFIDENCE COMES FROM CONSCIOUSLY NOTICING OUR RESISTANCE AND FEARS, LETTING GO OF THEM, AND THEN CHOOSING OUR BEST ACTION NOW.

Although sometimes we need to be disciplined and "just do it," most of the time we would be better off becoming more conscious before we act. When we act without consciousness, we create chaos in our own life as well as in the lives of those around us, whether we're at work or at home. Taking the time to become conscious leads us to greater confidence.

In business, I often notice that many leaders of companies quickly change the daily directions and priorities they communicate to their employees because of a fear-based reaction to some outside stimulus. This becomes very confusing and exhausting to employees, as they don't understand the reason for the new decision. They become unconscious of the direction of the company because their leaders are unconsciously reacting to situations and taking their employees off course.

Unconsciously reacting out of fear can result in any of the following:

- A client calls to demand delivery now and the boss tells an employee to drop his current project to meet this demand without any further consideration of other commitments.

- A new potential prospect demands instant attention and the boss, who was conducting a management meeting at the time of the call, leaves to take care of the prospect's question without hesitation, leaving the employees to sit and wonder what is going on.

- An employee quits and management reacts by expecting the other employees to figure out how they will now cover that employee's responsibilities, without trying to solve the problem or communicate to the employees about the situation.

There will always be outside stimuli calling for our attention, but if we are to be conscious and confident, we must take a moment to get curious, clear, and calm before we can become confident and choose the right action steps. Becoming confident is a discipline that requires us to dig down into our courage and stand in conscious observation of what is really happening around us, for a moment, before we act.

To become conscious and confident before we act, we must become aware of the inner blocks that are leading us astray from our inner wisdom. We stop being conscious and confident when our desire to see truth is overshadowed by a:

- *Fear* of some kind
- *Loss* of some kind
- *Shame* of some kind

Fear can come to us in the moment, causing us to lose our voice, our consciousness, and our confidence. For example, fear can arise in a meeting at work, when someone harshly disagrees with us. Our sudden thought could be, "Oh no! Was I wrong?" That feeling of fear could lead us further into a feeling of shame, as we jump to the next thought: "Oh, I was wrong. Did I look foolish?" It would be easy to then feel afraid that we could lose something and think, "Oh no! If I look foolish, will I lose the respect of everyone? Will I lose my job?"

With this chain reaction of thoughts and feelings, we can end up buried in one big pile of insecurity, wondering, "What happened to my confidence?" If we are not conscious about the state we are currently in, we could react to these thoughts by trying desperately to get ourselves out of this uncomfortable situation and the uncomfortable feelings of fear, loss, and shame.

Being confident means that we notice this part of ourselves that believes we need to be afraid of losing safety, security, love, and belonging, whether that translates to losing our job, a relationship, our reputation, our image, or a connection with money itself. When we are able to witness this aspect of our self, we can then confidently seek the best possible solutions for the situation by saying to ourselves, "Oh, isn't that interesting? That was a trigger, helping me to notice that I am attached to my reputation, my image, this relationship, that job, or this money. How might I best deal with this right now?"

Simply choose confidence: Consciously name the resistance that is causing you to feel insecure and self-doubt and then, "just do it."

WHEN WE ENGAGE IN A NEGATIVE BELIEF ABOUT OURSELVES, WE LOSE OUR CONFIDENCE AND BECOME DEFENSIVE.

When I was about 28 years old, I began my training and consulting business and found myself working with decision makers of companies that were often 20 years older than I was. Deep inside myself, I wondered, "Am I 'enough' to tell these men how to run their sales and marketing departments when I am just a girl, 20 years younger than they are? Why would they take me seriously?" I also told myself that it sure didn't help that I was a voluptuous blonde, but I tried my best to put aside these negative beliefs and maintain a state of confidence.

This self-doubt was secretly stirring inside of me, so that when these men would interrupt me, or harshly disagree with me, I would automatically feel disrespected and dishonored. It wasn't until I became conscious of my hidden beliefs about myself and began to respect and honor myself for the evolved and intelligent woman that I am that I could consistently feel confident and send out a different message through my emotional energy. This confidence, which I communicated through my body language, emotional energy, and tone of voice, made these same men change their attitudes and behavior toward me.

My confidence invited them to look at me differently. I didn't have to ignore their comments (that is, flee by avoiding taking action and simply allowing the behavior), nor did I have to fight to stop them (confront them abruptly). Instead, when they behaved in a way I found disrespectful, I simply paused, noticed it consciously, and focused on the inner thought, "I am worthy of your attention and respect right now." As I said this to myself,

I felt it, and sent it out to them nonverbally. Sending them this message altered our dynamic without my having to say anything.

You, too, can alter the dynamics of any interaction by first noticing the belief you hold about yourself in that situation or relationship. For example, if you are the parent of a teenager who is acting disrespectfully, deliberately disobeying you, ignoring you, or sassing you back, pause before reacting to them and ask yourself, "What do I believe I deserve from my child?" Notice whether you hold any beliefs about yourself as a parent that tell you that you deserve to be treated this way. Many parents who are divorced feel guilty about the divorce and deep down they believe that they deserve their child's disrespect. They don't realize that the child is acting disrespectful because at some level, she is asking them to teach her how to honor and respect others. It's important for the parent to put her own guilt aside and teach their teenager that lesson, regardless of whether or not the parent is divorced. To do this, the parent has to recognize his hidden belief and replace it with a positive one: "I deserve respect from my child."

In other cases, I've met employees who continually complain about their bosses and the company they work for because they feel undervalued. They wish that their boss would spend more time with them and more money on their department and when this doesn't happen, they feel stuck in their own insecurity and misery. Confident people in the same situation would notice their discontent and ask themselves, "How might I show the company the value my department has, and the effect we could have on the overall success of the company, if only they would invest more money in getting us much-needed equipment and personnel?"

Notice that in all of these examples, the first obstacle that has to be overcome is the inner belief "I am unworthy and deserve to be in this unpleasant situation." When we can identify the inner belief that is causing us to feel stuck, we can transform it, find our confidence, and take the necessary action to create a life that feels complete.

Discover your personal insecurities, which are caused by your secret negative beliefs about yourself. Then, let go of your self-doubt so that you can take action to get your needs met. Through the process of self-discovery, letting go, and action, you will find your confidence.

IT IS NORMAL TO FEEL INADEQUATE AT TIMES.

IT IS WHAT WE DO WITH THAT FEELING THAT CAN

MAKE US EXTRAORDINARILY CONFIDENT.

I remember hearing years ago that Johnny Carson claimed he always felt nervous right before he began his monologue on "The Tonight Show," even after he'd been hosting it for several years, but he just observed his feelings and did the show anyway. Most of us, just like Johnny Carson, have feelings of inadequacy that visit us from time to time. However, the difference between people who feel confident and people who do not has nothing to do with the feelings themselves. Instead, what matters is what they choose to do with their feelings of inadequacy.

When we recognize that it's normal to feel inadequate sometimes, we don't fear our feelings. Instead, we are able to go more deeply into them to understand them and transform them. If we don't explore them, they will become so big that we will feel small by comparison, and the result will be lingering feelings of inadequacy and a life that feels incomplete because we are not becoming all that we can be.

Don't be fooled into believing that an extremely confident person never feels a sense of inadequacy like you do. On the contrary! The truth is people like this have simply mastered the art of transforming their undesirable feelings into powerful thoughts that help them to access their confidence. Learning to notice our feelings of inadequacy, we can follow Johnny Carson's advice and, as the saying goes, "Feel the fear and do it anyway."

Our feelings of inadequacy often come up when we are stretching our comfort zone: trying something new, something we rarely do, something we aren't accustomed to, or something we believe we can't do. Because no one likes to feel inadequate, many of us will avoid stretching our comfort zone so that we don't have to feel this unpleasant feeling. Instead of stretching our comfort zone, we often choose complacency because while something in us is prompting us to stretch, another part of us is asking us to hold back out of fear, and that fear causes us to avoid taking action (flee) or fight (resisting change).

The best way to handle this situation is to breathe through your fear and find your confidence. To breathe through your fear, you have to find out where it is hiding in your body. Usually, you will find it in your belly area or around your heart and chest. To help move past your fear, you can also be clear with yourself (and others, too) that something you are facing is feeling big to you, while you are feeling small. I see this happen a lot when I am coaching employees who are new at a company. It doesn't matter how competent they are, how old they are, or how long they have been in a particular field. If they are new at the company, new in a position, or taking on a new strategic plan, they often find that their feelings of inadequacy have been triggered.

Instead of admitting our discomfort and then finding our confidence, we often mask our insecurities out of the fear that we will be judged by others if they discover that we are struggling to feel competent or worthy. Often, we're afraid to admit to ourselves that we are feeling insecure because we fear we might judge ourselves too harshly. Certainly at work, we fear that if we ever would reveal our insecurities, people might doubt our capabilities.

As you examine what your feelings are trying to tell you about yourself, you can clear out your self-doubt and heal. It is like pulling up old files on a computer, reading them, and deleting them to keep a clean hard drive so that you have more space. When you examine your self-doubt, ask yourself, "What is this feeling of inadequacy trying to tell me about what I believe about myself?"

One of my recent clients admitted feeling inferior to her partner, even though they started the business together. When they were strategically working on increasing revenue, she discovered that she had a knot in her stomach. In a coaching session, she mentioned it to me.

"What do you think that's about?" I asked her.

"I don't know for sure, but I'm worried that we won't be able to meet our goals."

"Who's 'we'?" I asked.

"Our sales force,' she said sheepishly.

"Hmm . . . you are the leader in this company, right?"

"Yes."

"Well, then, how do you feel about your ability to lead your salespeople, coach them, hold them accountable, and make the necessary decisions to meet the commitment of increasing your company's revenue?"

"Ohh . . . that's it!" she said. "I'm not sure I'm adequate for what would be required of me as a leader in this new situation where we're growing as a company. I know that I can see what needs to happen, but I get all frustrated and anxious and I end up approaching people like a nagging wife-'You're late,' 'You didn't meet your quota,' 'You're not focused!' Who wants to hear that?"

"Well, the good news is that you're admitting your feelings of inadequacy, and that's the first step," I said. "Now we just have to stretch your comfort zone, taking it a step or two further and developing your ability to be comfortable with your emotions. You need to feel energized and motivated to communicate with people to get them to help you solve problems, and you want to be able to hold them accountable to new strategies. Are you willing to learn some new personal leadership skills, so that you can lead others effectively?"

"I guess I will have to if I'm serious about meeting these goals."

"Good. Then the first step is for you to just take a personal inventory of how you feel when you see that things aren't going as you thought they ought to. Notice what you are saying about yourself and others, and use a journal to record what you're noticing, and then we'll talk more."

Ten days later, we met again and she gave me her journal. Her entries were about many different difficult situations that she felt were very big problems: a large account that she'd expected they would make a sale to didn't commit to a sale, salespeople didn't attend the sales meeting, a client expressed frustration with what he felt was inadequate customer service, departments were not being cooperative and following through on promises made to clients, etc. Mostly, she wrote about how frustrated she was with these people. She had disclosed little about how these situations left her feeling about herself or what she was saying to herself about herself regarding them.

"Besides frustrated, how did those situations leave you feeling?" I inquired.

"Pretty overwhelmed. Defeated. A bit hopeless at times," she answered.

"Okay, now let's take it to the next level. What did you tell yourself about yourself in those situations?"

"I'm not sure I said anything about myself to myself."

"Well, maybe not consciously, but there is a file stuck away somewhere inside you that has that information. You registered a judgment about yourself in that situation, or you wouldn't have felt 'overwhelmed, defeated, and a bit hopeless.' You see, it's our thoughts that create our feelings, not the circumstances or people around us."

"Hmm . . ." she said, reflecting on what I had just said. "I guess I probably said that I wasn't very good at conflict and didn't have time for all of this stuff."

"Good. What you are identifying is a feeling of 'not being enough,' a feeling of inadequacy. If you don't think you're good at conflict resolution, that means you feel inadequate trying to resolve conflicts harmoniously, right? Also, if you feel you don't have enough time, that indicates that you feel inadequate prioritizing, setting boundaries, and making good decisions for yourself based on your goals, right?"

"I guess so . . . but I never quite thought about it that way before."

The problem is that most of us prefer to blame our feelings on someone else. We hate to feel inadequate and would much prefer to feel like a victim of circumstances, so we focus on how other people are inadequate rather than face our own feelings of not being "enough." If we have the confidence to observe our feelings and learn from them, we can get rid the emotional muck that causes us to feel inadequate.

When it appears that something big is happening around you, check inside of yourself so that you can become clear about what is going on within you. Chances are that you are feeling inadequate in the moment. Noticing this feeling will help you to let it go and become confident again.

WE OFTEN USE BUSY-NESS TO HIDE OUR FEAR AND EMPTINESS. CONFIDENCE MEANS BEING WILLING TO SLOW DOWN AND GET CLEAR ABOUT WHAT WE WANT.

Recently, I spoke with a man who had to travel a lot in order to do his job. He was very financially successful and had been married since he was young, and had four beautiful children as well as a nice home in the suburbs. When I asked him how things were going, he mentioned how much he was traveling.

"Do you like to travel that much?" I asked.

"It's okay . . . It's just a little hard on my family, especially my wife," he replied.

"Do you see any light at the end of the tunnel?" I inquired.

"Not really. But we have a solid marriage, so I know we're just fine."

"That's good," I said, letting him know that I'd heard him. "How is your wife handling your being gone so much?"

"She's a bit depressed, so I've been trying to get her busy. I've suggested that she remodel our house, take a class, or maybe even go back to school."

"Hmm . . . that's interesting. What makes you suggest those things?" I wondered aloud.

"I just think she would be happier if she were busy! She has a lot of time on her hands right now, especially since our youngest is going away to college this year."

This conversation is similar to many that I have heard over the years. *Just get busy and ignore your own feelings! Just get busy and it (the issue) will go away!*

This is not to say the man wasn't a very caring husband. He just didn't take the time to slow down, explore his wife's feelings with her, and try to find out what she needed to do to feel better-

or what they needed to do as a couple to make adjustments for the good of the all.

Although sometimes being busy can be a good distraction, at other times, especially in the case of a life-altering transition such as this, it might be best to take some time to reflect and ask, "Now what? What should I do now?"

If we don't ask ourselves this question, we could miss a valuable opportunity to do something we longed to do that maybe we weren't even aware of. Perhaps we secretly want to take singing or dancing lessons, or write poetry, and yet we never allowed ourselves to think about our dream, much less share it with our significant other.

Thinking about all of this, I challenged him on his approach.

"Might you both consider slowing down and spending more time exploring why she is depressed and what she needs to do about it, instead of encouraging her to just get busy?"

"I don't know what good that will do. I know when I slow down, I'm riddled with guilt, and the problem is, nothing about my life can change, so I just end up feeling more anxious. As for my wife, the more she thinks about it, the more she gets depressed. We both knew what we were getting into when I took on this career and this job in particular, so I think the best solution is for her to just get busier and then she won't feel so alone."

Although I really understood what his logic was telling him, I could also see the impulsiveness in his thinking. Unfortunately, when we do slow down enough to feel our emotions, our mind will often race or be weighted down by heavy thoughts. This initial feeling can keep us from wanting to slow down. However, if we can go further into our feeling self, just long enough to ask clear questions and listen to the answers, we can then be confident that we are choosing the best solutions to deal with the situation.

Questions that can help you to become confident about your decisions include:

- "Hmm . . . I wonder why I am feeling guilty (anxious, depressed, etc.) about slowing down?"
- "How is this situation familiar to me? Does it remind me of a childhood experience?"
- "What did I tell myself about myself in my past, that I might still be telling myself now?"
- "What do I need to do now to feel better?"

If we just get busy and avoid this inner dialog, we will most likely find ourselves suffering from insomnia or perhaps experiencing other side effects of our self-avoidance.

When I work with people at this deeper emotional level, even in the workplace, it is interesting to see what comes up that requires healing. Like the wife in the scenario above, a man at a company was experiencing loneliness and sadness, only he was experiencing it at work when his boss was out traveling. My client admitted that he felt not only alone, but unworthy of his boss's attention. He felt jealous that "something out there" was capturing his boss's attention and not him, thus leaving him feeling "not enough" and unworthy. When he became open enough for us to explore these feelings, and get beyond his depression and anxiety, he realized the unlimited possibilities of perceiving the situation differently. Getting busy was not the solution. Seeing the situation differently was. Instead of seeing his busy boss as not caring about him (which was what he used to think was true about his busy parent), he could now see his busy boss as being overcommitted and overwhelmed. This brought him back to a state of confidence about the choices he could make to connect with his boss.

Unfortunately, there is no easy shortcut in this self-discovery process. The only way out of the anxiety and depression is through the lie we told ourselves that got us there to begin with. When we try to avoid the negative feelings by covering up our inner lie with Pollyannaish thinking or busy-ness, we simply put a Band-Aid on a wound that will continue to get worse if left unattended.

Slow down and get clear about what you are feeling so that you can discover what it is that you want, and thus become confident in your decision making.

PRACTICE GETTING CONFIDENT,

AND YOU WILL BECOME CONFIDENT.

Just as with anything else in life, when it comes to confidence, practice makes perfect! Below you will find ten things you can do to build your confidence muscle and achieve the fourth piece of the personal leadership puzzle:

1. *Bless the more fearful aspect of yourself for wanting to protect you.*

   We often have a fearful aspect of ourselves that has held us back in order to protect us from feeling unloved, unsafe, and inadequate. When we grow and let go of our attachments to particular outcomes, we no longer need to hold on to our fear to protect us. If you are ready to grow, notice your fear, bless it for protecting you all these years, and kindly tell it, "You are no longer needed." This will help you to make room for your more confident self.

2. *Use the power of positive thinking and visualization. Recite affirmations to yourself and see yourself as big and confident.*

   Being aware that thoughts create feelings and images in our mind can help us to create confidence. Positive self-talk and positive visualization are key elements in confidence building. In fact, many people find that emulating someone who is confident can help them to feel confident, so they visualize themselves behaving in the confident manner of someone they admire.

3. *Become more confident by magnifying your strengths, minimizing your weaknesses, and growing from your experiences.*

   Accentuate the positive in yourself and others! When we live with this viewpoint, we achieve a state of confidence, seeing any challenging situation as a glass half full, a lemon we can turn into lemonade, or a lesson we can learn from. To become more confident, practice accentuating the positive.

4. *Observe the controlling part of you that is fearful. Love yourself unconditionally as you grow more open, trusting, and allowing.*

   Confident people make decisions out of love, not fear. They are able to trust in themselves and to trust that what they need and desire will come to them. How freeing it is to let go of our fear and our feeling that we have to control everything and everyone around us in order to be happy! If being more trusting is difficult for you, begin by noticing the fearful aspect of yourself that believes you need to control every conversation, every person, and everything around you for you to be okay. Just notice and watch to see how life unfolds when you are the spectator, open to whatever happens.

5. *Keep a Confidence Journal. Remember the times that your confidence helped you to feel complete.*

   Whether your confidence came from saying no when you meant it, or saying yes when you meant it, or it came from stretching your comfort zone and trying something new, the more you can remember how great it feels to be confident, the more you will want to engage in the thoughts and behaviors that will get you there again in the future. Creating a

Confidence Journal can help you do just that. Write down these experiences in a journal by stating the situation, what your fear was initially, and what behavior you would have chosen if you would've let your fear control you. Then write down what you told yourself about the situation or yourself that allowed you to find your confidence and choose a more desirable behavior. Note what outcome you got as a result of this transformation.

6. *Build your confidence on a daily basis. Identify what you need and ask others for exactly what you need.*

   Confident people are clear about who they are and what they need and do not hesitate to share their needs and feelings with others. If this is difficult for you, begin by practicing in small arenas. You might go to a restaurant and ask the waitress for the "extras" you really want. Or, practice with the people you are most comfortable with in your life, and then, once you've had some practice and built some confidence, expand your asking by approaching people you aren't so comfortable with and telling them what you'd like them to do for you.

7. *Set realistic goals and follow through on meeting them.*

   Just as confident people ask for what they need, they also go after what they want. Setting realistic goals can help you to do that. When you work on your goals, you become confident because you're giving yourself the message that you could and that your goals matter.

8. *Continue to build your confidence by being courageous. Stretch your comfort zone.*

   We build confidence by stretching our comfort zone and meeting challenges we weren't sure we could meet. These experiences allow us to see parts of ourselves that we did not know existed. Find an interest that you have never tried before. Pursue it. Feel your fear and then the exhilaration and eventual confidence that comes from stretching your comfort zone.

9. *Be confident as you face difficulties and opposition using a three-pronged approach of assessing, feeling, and strategizing.*

   Assess what is happening and how you feel, then strategize so you can take action. This three-pronged approach will help you to feel connected and confident as you create the life you want because you will not be ignoring clues that you need to pay attention to a certain situation. Confident people notice what is required in a given situation and, after assessing what needs to be done, move quickly to take action.

10. *Results build confidence: Carve out time every day to make your dreams and goals come true. Find the "little wasted moments" and take advantage of them.*

    Often, we think we do not have enough time to make our dreams come true. Instead of feeling like a victim to the "time monster" that eats up all of your time, be proactive and carve out time every day to make your dreams come true. Notice the wasted moments that you spend giving in to meaningless distractions and other activities that are less important to you.

> *Practice the ten steps to confidence to prepare yourself for the next piece of the personal leadership puzzle, which is to get caring!*

FIFTH PIECE:

GET CARING! OPEN YOUR HEART TO LOVE

As we commit to a life of personal leadership, we learn that the fifth piece, get caring, helps us to sustain and continue to build the life we desire more easily than we could if we were operating out of fear. When we are operating out of caring and love instead of fear, it seems that we can get more miles per gallon and can go the extra mile when necessary.

In order to continue our journey in personal leadership, we must open our heart to that which we care about. When we care about something or someone-whether it be a business, a friendship, a child-parent relationship, a significant other, our health, or a philanthropic concern-we tend to pay closer attention to it and put more energy into it.

To get caring means being willing to open ourselves up to a cause or person and risk being a fool for love. Being a fool for love means we are unattached to the outcome of a given situation and are more focused on the cause we care about or the person's best interest. For example, you might care deeply about your child and know that your teenager is currently upset with you because you will not let him stay over night at a co-ed homecoming sleepover, as other parents might be doing. You have made this decision out of love for your child, weighing your family's values and what you believe your child can tolerate. Although you do not like that your child is currently angry with you, you can let go of that outcome and focus on what you believe is in the best interest of your child.

To get caring means we attend to those people and things we love, but it does not mean we become a caretaker to everyone, attending to their every need and concern, or letting others take advantage of us. It means we are able to care for ourselves as we care for others, with the highest good of all in mind.

In fact, the more we are aware of ourselves and care for ourselves, the better we can care for others. This is true because we are able to have a true connection with and empathy for another person or cause. We understand their feelings and needs because we are so aware of our own.

DISAPPOINTMENTS OFTEN KEEP US FROM CARING.

When we're not caring, we can become very pessimistic. As they are sharing their inner experiences with me, my clients will often say, "It's so easy to go through the motions in life and be half present, waiting for the other shoe to drop."

"Doesn't sound like a whole lot of fun," is usually what I say in return, and although they laugh, we all understand that it is easier said than done to let go of pessimism and the fear of being disappointed.

The fear of being disappointed can keep us from opening our heart and pursuing with wild abandon what it is we really want. Even if we do experience our courage for a while, something in us feels the need to be on guard, just waiting for something negative to jump out at us around the corner. We are afraid of being found out, finding something out, coming up short, or becoming a fool for love.

This fear of disappointment can show up in all areas of our life, at work and at home. We can be afraid we will disappoint our boss or co-worker or that they will disappoint us. At home, we might find our spouse's or child's behavior disappointing on a regular basis, or believe we can never quite measure up to someone else's standards.

Disappointment can paralyze us and prevent us from caring about anything because most of our energy is going toward thinking about that which we fear. Or, if that is not the case, we become shut down in the face of someone's else's disappointment with us. Waiting and wondering if we will be disappointed or disappoint someone else robs us of the joy that is available to us in the present moment. Something in us would rather be right than happy, so we will choose to spend all week long waiting and anticipating that moment when we will be disappointed, and reassuring ourselves that when it does happen, at least we will be able to say to ourselves, "See? I was right! I knew that would happen!"

We have another choice. We could get caring and feel joyous while things are happening as we'd hoped, and if we should get disappointed or become a disappointment to someone else, we could recognize the disappointment, humble ourselves, and deal with it.

A client of mine had asked me to work with one of his vice presidents, who seemed distracted and less than motivated in his job. The owner was growing more disappointed in this vice president's performance and assumed the problem was that his employee no longer cared about his job, for one reason or another. After I met with the vice president several times, he shared with me what the real problem was, telling me, "I'm having troubles with my wife. I've been disappointed over the years at her lack of response to me. It seems as if we don't connect anymore and all I hear from her is a list of what she's disappointed about. For years, she accused me of having an affair when I traveled. Honestly, I hadn't cheated on her. I was also having issues at work because I felt that I could never measure up to my boss's standards. No matter what I tried to do at work or at home, it seemed that I was a disappointment to everyone. On top of it all, my son, who is sixteen, has been a disappointment to me, too. He keeps getting bad grades in school and was recently caught using drugs. Everywhere I turn, it's a disappointment. Then, when I was out of town once, in a city that I travel to regularly, I met a woman who was a lot of fun. After years of hearing accusations of cheating and not feeling any joy in my marriage, I was weak. This woman and I starting to see each other, but I'm confused and afraid. I don't want to break up my family and disappoint everyone . . . . "

This story, of one disappointment after another shows us that if we wallow in our disappointments, we can miss the opportunity to get caring and dig deeper into the real reason behind our disappointment. If we have the courage to look at our disappointment, we can begin to resolve our issues and regain our sense of joy.

Let's break down the scenario above and show how getting caring could work to overcome disappointment:

- "I'm having troubles with my wife. I've been disappointed over the years at her lack of response to me. It seems as if we don't connect anymore and all I hear from her is a list of what she's disappointed about."

  Life coach response: *Instead of wallowing in disappointment, how about going to your wife and saying, "I've noticed we don't connect like we used to anymore. I hear your disappointment in me and want to sit down and really discuss what it is you need from me, so that I can care for you. I think we can get reconnected if we focus on how we might care for each other better." (Although this conversation would not guarantee immediate results, if he would focus on his desire and intention to get caring and become open to her feelings and needs, they might eventually resolve their conflicts harmoniously).*

- "For years she accused me of having an affair when I traveled. Honestly, I hadn't cheated on her. . . . After years of hearing accusations of cheating and not having any joy in our relationship, I became weak."

  Life coach response: *Instead of wallowing in disappointment, he could have gotten caring and been direct and honest with her about her accusations and concerns. He could have done this by saying, "I understand that it must be hard for you to be alone when I travel. I also understand that the idea of me being away and potentially being in the company of another woman must be frightening to you. What can I do to help you feel more secure about yourself and us as a couple? I'm afraid if we keep at each other like this that we'll grow apart, and then our marriage will be more vulnerable to an affair and I don't want that to happen." (Again, this wouldn't have guaranteed her participation in a healthy conversation, but it certainly would have invited it. If he can be patient while she discovers what she feels and what she needs, and continue this statement as a mantra in the meantime, their chance of success is greater).*

- "I was also having issues at work because I felt that I could never measure up to my boss' standards. No matter what I tried to do at work or at home, it seemed that I was a disappointment to everyone."

  Life coach response: *Instead of wallowing in disappointment, he could let his boss know how much he cares by saying, "I've noticed lately that I'm coming up short in your eyes. I want you to know that I'm truly concerned about the welfare of the company, and if I'm disappointing you, perhaps it's because I'm not clear about what you need and expect. Can we sit down and discuss how I might perform to your standards?"*

  (While it's possible that the boss may be demanding, impossible, and incapable of being satisfied, this would still be a fruitful conversation to have because it is direct and specific. If the boss would continue to be

unsatisfied after numerous attempts to understand, then the employee could conclude that he just doesn't fit well with the boss).

- "On top of it all, my son, who is sixteen, has been a disappointment to me, too. He keeps getting bad grades in school and was recently caught using drugs."

  Life coach response: *Instead of wallowing in disappointment, he could get caring and approach his son to explore the son's perspective and dilemma. Practicing the first steps of the personal leadership puzzle would help him to first get curious, clear, calm, and confident. Then he could get caring and approach his son. (We cannot control anyone else's destiny because we all live by free will and have our lessons to learn. However, this caring approach would certainly welcome greater healing and connection between father and son.)*

- "Everywhere I turn, it's a disappointment. Then, when I was out of town once, in a city that I travel to regularly, I met a woman who was a lot of fun. . . . This woman and I started to see each other, but I'm confused and afraid. I don't want to break up my family and disappoint everyone."

  Life coach response: *Chances are that if the above steps had been taken, the scenario would have never gotten this far. However, let's say it did. Instead of wallowing in disappointment, the man could go to his wife and say, "I feel we are really growing apart, to the point that I feel vulnerable. Perhaps you do, too. I would like us to take a serious look at our relationship, before it's too late, and rediscover the love we once felt for each other. How might we do that?" (This doesn't guarantee that his wife would not just walk out the door at that moment, or begin questioning him about what he meant by "vulnerable," but if he could stay curious, clear, calm, confident, and caring, he could help his wife shift into the important question, which is, "How might we save this marriage?").*

When we address our disappointments and those of others, one at a time, we have a better chance of caring and resolving potential issues.

Notice when disappointment appears within you and around you. See it as an opportunity to care. Remember: It's not disappointment itself that's the problem. The real problem is our fear of disappointment, our lack of humility, and our inability to deal with other people's disappointment with us. Instead of avoiding disappointment, name it and resolve it quickly and you will feel caring once again.

TO GET CARING MEANS WE STOP AND WONDER, "HOW MIGHT I CARE FOR OTHERS, AS I CARE FOR MYSELF?"

It's human nature for us to wonder, "What's in it for me?" and "What could I do to make myself feel important in this situation?", but when we are committed to personal leadership, we notice this tendency in ourselves and go beyond it to find the fifth piece of the personal leadership puzzle: get caring. Getting caring makes us feel fulfilled and complete because we include others in the equation as we consider our options.

You can easily see what people care about by watching their behavior. Say, for example, that you go to a restaurant and want to customize your order-you ask for your dressing on the side of your salad, pickles on the hamburger and not on the side, and fruit instead of fries. Watch and listen to how your waitress handles these requests. If her focus is on what's in it for you and making you feel important, she will make sure she understood what you wanted. She will smile and repeat your requests. If she is wondering what is in it for her, or wants you to make her feel important, she will probably listen half-heartedly to your request, be in a hurry, and think to herself, "Oh boy, now I have to work harder!" Her concern for her own convenience over serving you what you wanted might be very obvious: She might sigh out loud, expressing her frustration.

We see this uncaring behavior everywhere around us, including at home. Teenagers are notorious for being concerned about what is in it for them and wanting to feel important. This is evident when you stop giving to them and ask for something in return. For example, you can buy your child a car so that he can get himself back and forth from his activities, but when you ask him to do something for the family, like take the car in for an emissions test, you will get to see if he is deeply entrenched in the "what's in it for me/make me feel important" syndrome or if he is at a point in his development where he can include others in the "care-equation." If he is not at the point where he can give as he receives, this could be a great opportunity to chat with him about the concept of "what's good for the all," so he can learn about the fifth piece in the leadership puzzle: get caring.

At work, we often see people who are stuck in the "what's in it for me/make me feel important" syndrome:

- Your co-worker or assistant doesn't go the extra mile for you and finish a project before the end of the day as you requested.

- A team member doesn't complete a project as promised.

- Your boss doesn't take the time to explain to you the changes that are happening with a client, even though you are the primary customer service contact for the customer.

Just because someone does or doesn't do these things doesn't mean they don't care about you. It just means they are in the "what's in it for me/make me feel important" syndrome and, as a result, they miss opportunities to get caring.

To get caring doesn't mean we always bend over backwards to meet everyone's needs. It does mean we care enough to communicate when we can't, letting them know when we don't have enough time, or that a change has taken place that will affect them, or that their request or needs aren't a priority for us right now. Taking the time to communicate shows others that we care.

We can end up in a cycle of uncaring behavior ourselves

when we are disappointed by others' uncaring behavior. Instead of getting curious about what is really going on so that we can be clear, calm, confident, and caring as we approach them, we can tell ourselves all sorts of uncaring things about that other person and say to ourselves judgmental things such as, "He isn't a team player!" or "He doesn't respect me!" when the other person's behavior is really not about us at all-it is all about that person not feeling important and not being able to get beyond himself enough to see what's in it for someone else and how he might get caring.

We react by wanting to judge our offender because we are focused on needing to feel important ourselves and because we are so concerned about what is in it for ourselves that we take the other person's behavior personally. When we quickly scan the situation, focused on our importance and what is in it for us, we miss the opportunity to get caring.

A client of mine shared with me an opportunity he had to get caring. He had noticed that his wife was drinking more than usual at night when she got home from work. When he would observe this behavior in the past, he would hide in his library and get busy with reading or working on the computer. After we had several coaching sessions that focused on connecting with people from a caring heart, at work and at home, he saw the situation as an opportunity to connect out of caring and decided to use the opportunity rather than fleeing from it and giving in to judgment.

Looking at his wife's drinking differently, he approached her lovingly and told her that he noticed she had been drinking at home alone on a more regular basis. He asked, "What is that about for you?"-a question I taught him in coaching that could be used with anyone when we want to avoid being judgmental and instead be curious and caring. To his surprise, when he asked this question, she began to talk about some of her own difficulties at work and her fear about growing old and becoming unwanted. He said that initially, just staying in the present moment, listening to her and caring about her without feeling a need to fix her problems, give advice, or flee because he was afraid he couldn't handle it properly, was really hard. Then, he said, he remembered something I had said in a session when we were talking about what his employees really wanted when they were complaining to him. He said he remembered me saying,

"When your employees are complaining to you, they don't care how much you know, they care how much you care. Stop trying to fix things or taking other people's bad behavior personally and learn how to get caring through the use of empathy. Put yourself in their shoes and feel what it feels like to be in their position. Let them know you can feel what it feels like, from their perspective."

Remembering this tip on empathy, he said he knew that all he really had to do was to keep his heart open to love as he listened to her concerns. The more he focused on just listening in love, the easier it got.

After that night, the two of them began to take evening walks together after work and share in the day's stresses with one another, offering each other a caring presence and giving advice only when it was asked for. When I asked, "What was the best thing about that experience for you?", he answered, "Getting beyond myself and my own fear about where her drinking might take her. See, my mom was an alcoholic and my initial reaction was to fear that I was going to end up in the same situation again, with a person who was going to become unavailable because she was drowning in alcohol. Instead of staying with that thought and potentially watching it happen to me all over again, I got caring about what was going on with her. Because I got caring, we were able to connect and prevent things from getting worse. Not only was I caring for her, but by choosing to get beyond my fear and get caring, I was caring for me, too."

Stop thinking only about making yourself feel important or being concerned only about what's in it for you, and ask the other person, "What is that about for you?" This question will help you focus on how you might care for others as you care for yourself.

IT IS IMPORTANT TO CARE FOR OURSELVES FIRST, SO THAT WE CAN OPERATE FROM A PLACE OF "LOVE OVERFLOW." THAT WAY, WE TRULY CARE, AND OUR CARING COMES FROM THE ABUNDANT LOVE WITHIN US.

"Love others as you love yourself." This belief is central to Judeo/Christian tradition, yet it is one of the most misunderstood concepts around. What does it mean, exactly?

When we take the time to fill ourselves up with love, by caring for ourselves deeply, we experience "love overflow," creating an abundance of love that we can give away to others.

Loving ourselves first might include:

- Getting more sleep.
- Getting more emotional rest.
- Making more time for personal reflection.
- Making choices that are congruent with our heart's desire instead of doing things out of obligation.
- Getting more physical exercise.
- Getting more balance between work and play, helping others and helping ourselves.
- Having more fun.

The Biblical story of Martha and Mary is an example of how to get caring by taking care of yourself first. Martha was the epitome of the superwoman, overworked and under cared for, and always giving. Martha worked very hard to make things perfect for everyone but herself, and as a result, became quickly annoyed when things didn't go her way. In the story, she is attending to all the obligations in her home as Jesus relaxes and talks to her sister, Mary.

Like a martyr, Martha complains about Mary not pulling her weight like she is, only to hear from Jesus that she needs to relax, like Mary, and stop focusing on distractions.

Mary, meanwhile, is sitting with Jesus, delighting in His company and making Him feel important. She is focusing on what's in it for Him and what He wants from her rather than running around like Martha who is trying desperately to impress everyone, and failing miserably because she is operating more from her own fear of failure than her real love for Him.

When we are giving and giving in order to make a good impression, our giving is not caring because it is all about us. Our giving becomes an empty ritual. Empty rituals can include:

- Sending a thank you card, only because it is the right thing to do, when we do not feel thankful at all.

- Sending expensive flowers and presents on the appropriate occasions instead of not taking the time to wonder, "What would really make this person feel loved and special?"

To get caring means we are connecting deeply with ourselves first, so that we give from the heart. For example, we might attend a barbecue where the weather isn't what the forecast said it would be, the chicken got overdone on the grill, and someone forgot to bring the ketchup, yet everyone leaves feeling really cared for anyway because the host or hostess was more like a Mary than a Martha, connecting with the guests and making them feel important.

Obviously, in an ideal world, we like to have the sun shining, the meal perfect, and everyone remembering to bring the condiments they promised to bring. But when that doesn't happen, how will we choose to respond to it? Caring is an act of an open heart, and it does not require a perfect situation.

A recent situation reminded me of the importance of acting like a Mary versus Martha. It was a rainy summer night and my friend and I decided to go out for dinner to a new and expensive steak house downtown. Our first impression, after only sitting down for a few minutes, was that the restaurant was extremely cold and uncomfortable. We complained to the waiter and within five minutes, even though the restaurant was extremely busy, the maitre d' came to us to apologize and said that they would turn down the air conditioning immediately.

Then, my friend ordered her favorite wine only to find out they didn't carry it, although their advertisements bragged about having the largest wine cellar in the area. Again, the waiter took the time to apologize and suggested another wine option, at no charge. She was so impressed by their care, in spite of their imperfection, that she brought her ten employees back there one month later for a customer service experiential outing!

We later found out that the owner had always dreamed of having this type of restaurant and obviously was giving out of his love overflow and desire to share with others a wonderful dining experience. A long period of wishing, wanting, and caring prepared him to have enough love overflow for the hurdles he experienced during his first opening weeks.

Create a "love overflow" for yourself. It will allow you to get caring even in the most difficult circumstances.

WHEN WE RISK DISCOVERING WHAT FEELS LOVING TO OTHERS, WE CAN GIVE UP OPERATING FROM A SCRIPT AND GET CARING!

In his book *The Five Languages of Love*, Dr. Gary Chapman discusses the importance of speaking the love language of the person we are in a relationship with so that we do not waste time and effort operating from a "love-script" that we conjured up in our minds. The five love languages he speaks of are:

1) *Verbal affirmation:* This includes sharing your positive feelings with someone, including how you feel about them and what you think is great about them. It may sound like: "I believe in you!," "You make me smile," or "You are such a great cook."

2) *Quality time:* This means spending time with someone, creating memories as you engage in activities that they like to do, and spending the amount of time together that they like to spend.

3) *Special gifts:* This would include anything that would demonstrate that the person thought of you, knows you, or wants to invest money in you. It could include flowers, jewelry or any type of present in material form.

4) *Acts of kindness, service, and help:* This is love expressed in gestures such as bringing you breakfast in bed, doing a chore of yours, helping you out with a responsibility, and so on.

5) *Physical affection:* This is any form of physical connection, ranging from a twinkle in your eye, to a pat on the shoulder, to a more intimate form of physical expression.

A person who is in tune with your needs, feelings, and boundaries around these forms of love it is able to give to you according to your love language.

Steven Covey, the author of *The Seven Habits of Highly Effective People*, says in his book, "Seeking to understand another, is the greatest human desire." When you combine his philosophy with Dr. Gary Chapman's, you have a recipe for how to get caring.

To get caring means that we get beyond our own preconceived notions of what makes us feel important and cared for and seek to find out what makes someone else feel that way. If we don't do that, we can waste a lot of time, money, and energy and end up wondering why our efforts are not paying off.

After dating a gentleman for only a few weeks, I broke off the relationship because I could see that we had very different languages of love. He had known me for only a few weeks, and offered to clean out my messy garage, an act of kindness and service that he felt was very loving. Even though I had an overflow of boxes from a move I had made just months before, I kindly declined his offer, told him that my lawn maintenance man was going to take care of it next spring and that I would rather spend quality time getting to know him. After he made several attempts to coerce me into letting him organize my garage, I finally gave in with two conditions: that he would allow me to pay for the shelving he was suggesting I get and that we would only spend one afternoon on the garage, and after that, let the rest go for my maintenance man to take care of.

Well, the gentleman spent one afternoon on the project with me and it did not get done, so he continued to bring me things to finish off the garage and insist on our spending time organizing it together. I decided to get curious, and asked him about his need to help me clean my garage. He shared with me that he thought organizing space was a great experience to share together and that it made him feel as if we were a team, working side-by-side. The harder I tried to explain that it wasn't a good experience for me, and that I preferred to hire and pay someone to do the job, the more he insisted on doing it for me. Even though I had actually come down with a sinus infection because of working in all of the dust floating around the garage, and complained about how cleaning it was ruining my nails, he still insisted that by working with me to organize my garage, he was performing an act of love for me.

I tried really hard not to psychoanalyze him, but I must tell you that I wondered if he was a bit O.C.D. (people with O.C.D., which stands for Obsessive Compulsive Disorder, often have a strong psychological need to clean). Having compassion for him, I waited it out for another few weeks to see if it was just my garage that was driving him nuts or if his seeming obsession with cleaning my garage was part of a pattern of avoiding getting to know me and what my real needs and desires are.

Within a few weeks, I could see that it was the latter when Valentine's Day rolled around and he bought me his favorite perfume for women. I found this very odd, since I had just shared how a few months previously, my daughters had surprised me by buying me my favorite perfume. In telling him the story, I had gone into great detail about their thoughtfulness, and expressed how much I appreciated their surprising me with this gift I had wanted. When I asked him what made him decide to buy the perfume he chose for me, he answered, "Because I liked it, researched it, and found out it's a popular perfume!"

Needless to say that when I told him this relationship wasn't working for me, he didn't get it. He said he felt that he had given so much and couldn't understand why I couldn't accept his kind gestures. I told him that his kind gestures didn't have anything to do with getting to know me and that, in fact, they seemed more about him and his need to please. I reminded him that I had explained to him again and again that being the independent woman that I am, I am pretty clear about how I like things done in my home and what I like to wear, including my perfume. I said that what I really wanted from a relationship was to spend quality time getting to know someone and having them get to know me.

When it comes to the workplace, I advise my clients that they, too, should get to know what makes someone feel important and special, and not make assumptions. Many managers, wanting to show employees they care, think that if they just take an employee to lunch, buy him a gift, or give him a bonus, the employee will know he is appreciated. I have seen many company leaders spend hours trying to come up with the "best" incentive programs, only to fail because they forgot to ask their employees what *they* wanted. Maybe they wanted more face time with the boss (quality time), or a specific expression of appreciation (verbal affirmation), or to be allowed to go home early one night (act of kindness). Tuning in to what that person's love language is can make a huge difference in helping them realize that we care.

When you are looking to make the best decision about how to care for someone else, I suggest you consider this formula:

The best decisions = the solutions + the buy-in

If you think your solution is the best decision, but you don't ask the person if he agrees, chances are that you will be wrong. Whether it is at work or at home, find out what makes people feel that you care. When it comes to the workplace, obviously, expressing appreciation with physical affection has its limits, but a mere pat on the back or a direct look in the eye with a handshake of congratulations can mean a lot to the person who feels cared for when he or she receives physical affection.

When it comes to our children, we can easily overindulge them and assume we are being caring when we attend every one of their activities, buy them the best and the latest everything, and make sure we are waiting on them hand and foot. Again, we need to be curious, clear, calm, confident, and caring about our giving. Is it for them, and their highest good, that we are giving to them, or are we doing it to satisfy our own need to feel good about ourselves?

I remember one time when my daughter was twelve and had come home after being at her friend's house after school. She had expressed how nice it was that the mom had served them tea and cute little tea breads with a spread of some sort on them, and had brought them into her daughter's bedroom where they were, serving the snack on China dishes. My first reaction was to say, "And your point is?" Her comeback was clear, calm, and confident. "I would like if you would do that for me and my friends some time." Again, I couldn't believe my ears. Wasn't it enough that I was a single mom supporting my family, and available after school for my girls, so they could have quality time with me? Now I had to throw tea parties for them, as well? Of course, since spending quality time with those I love was my language of love, I thought doing that was most important, and that any other expression of love wasn't necessary.

After getting over my initial "ego tantrum," I decided to get to know my child a little better. She was telling me that an act of service was her language of love. The funny part was that acts of service were the hardest things for me to do, and therefore, an act of service would truly be an act of selfless love on my part.

Although I did not often bring her tea and tea breads for her friends, I did find out other little ways to show her I cared through little acts of kindness, which is what she was really asking for. I made some of our favorite family recipes when her friends would come over, or took them to special places they wanted to go, and performed other special acts of kindness that I knew would make her feel cared for.

There were also times that getting caring meant saying *no*. For example, when my youngest came home and complained that all the other kids had new cars and hers was the oldest of them all, I got caring by engaging in empathetic listening. I knew that it must be hard growing up in an affluent neighborhood in an age of entitlement. In this case, I reminded her that I chose to not indulge her with too many gifts, not because I couldn't afford it, but because I wanted her to grow up and appreciate the value of money, hard work, and material things, and recognize that possessions are less important than connections of the heart. By the time she was nineteen, three years later, she thanked me for that lesson, as she looked back during her first year of college and cherished our many fabulous memories together.

Dare to discover what makes others feel cared for and honor their language of love even as you honor your own.

GET CARING BY KNOWING WHEN TO CHOOSE TOUGH LOVE.

When I think about tough love, I think of the countless examples of Jesus in the Bible. Among the Biblical examples of tough love are:

- Jesus knew not to speak when someone's heart was hard and wouldn't be able to hear Him anyway. He advised us, "Don't give pearls to a swine" to remind us that sometimes, the most loving thing to do is to say nothing, especially when someone will not hear you anyway.

- Jesus confronted people and "spoke the truth in love." He told the people who were getting ready to stone the adulteress, "He who is without sin must cast the first stone," confronting them on their judgment of her, when they, too, were sinners.

- He told the Pharisees that they were acting like hypocrites and said, "Some of you will call me by name, and I will say, 'Away with you.' I will know my people by the fruit of their Spirit."

- He also told his disciple, Peter, that despite Peter's claims of loyalty, he would betray Him three times before the night was over, and sure enough, Peter did.

For me, Jesus is the greatest example of caring. He doesn't care in order to be liked or accepted; he cares because He is concerned about our best interests. If speaking the truth in love was what someone needed, that is what He did for them, and what He continues to do for us now, through the still, small voice that resides in us.

Some people question the love of God when they face the difficulties of their own life and today's world condition. They question, "Why would a good God allow such pain in my life and in the world?" I believe a good God allows pain for the purpose of gain.

I've observed many examples of how people are capable of becoming better and kinder after experiencing pain. After 9/11, people in New York City were much nicer to visitors, now appreciating how tourism helped their economy; business owners reevaluated their quest to expand at all costs; and families drew closer, reevaluating their lives and priorities.

I don't believe God likes bad things to happen to us, but I do believe He allows bad things to happen so that He can draw our attention back to Him, and to push us to get caring about what really matters instead of our daily concerns and our attachments to safety, security, love, and belonging.

When I think of tough love, I also think of the word "accountability." Accountability is something I taught my children when they were growing up and that I now I teach in the workplace. I often see clients who become dissatisfied with their employees and instead of practicing tough love by coaching them and holding them accountable to a higher standard, they wait until the situation is so bad that they fire them. They feel that somehow, speaking the truth in love is not nice. I think it is not nice to suddenly let someone go without giving them an opportunity for growth.

I see this problem in parenting, too. Many times, a parent does not sit down and talk to her children about the issues she sees in their lives and in their character. Instead, I hear about parents who say nothing and then suddenly get mad when their child starts behaving in an undesirable way. To practice tough love and get caring means being willing to take the time to talk with someone, seek to understand where they are stuck, speak the truth in love, and offer correction and accountability where needed.

Practice tough love when it's needed. You can do this by speaking the truth in love and allowing for difficult circumstances to wake people up and redirect them. Remember: Tough love is a key element in getting caring.

SIXTH PIECE:

GET COMMITTED! OVERCOME OBSTACLES

Commitment, the sixth piece of the personal leadership puzzle, is a state of mind that keeps us bound emotionally or intellectually to a course of action or to another person or persons, despite obstacles. When we are committed, we operate from a positive belief system that allows us to persevere even in the most difficult situations. We are able to be open about what we need and feel and we are able to allow things to unfold as they need to in perfect timing, while we remain steadfast.

If we are to stay committed, we must hold in our mind our vision of the long-term outcome, knowing that there will be many bumps in the road along the way. When we are committed, obstacles do not hold us back. If we encounter one, we simply ask ourselves, "How might I remove this obstacle so that I can get back on course?" versus saying, "Oh, this is getting hard. Should I really be doing this?"

When we get committed to a cause or a person, we focus on the possibilities before us instead of wasting vital energy changing our minds and second guessing ourselves all the time, asking whether or not we should be in a particular relationship or situation. We take that energy and focus it on a solution, asking ourselves, "How might I make this work?" We achieve the results we desire because we persevere despite the obstacles.

WHEN WE HOLD OURSELVES AND OTHERS ACCOUNTABLE TO THE COMMITMENTS THAT HAVE BEEN MADE, WE HELP THEM TO OVERCOME OBSTACLES.

Sometimes, we just don't feel the passion or enthusiasm we once did when we first committed to something or someone in our life, before we came across all the bumps in the road and disappointments along the way. It is in this stage of personal leadership that we can embrace the sixth piece: get committed. We need to hold ourselves and others accountable to the commitments we and others have made, and despite any obstacles, "just do it." The original feelings of passion will reappear as we resolve the day-to-day issues and disappointments we encounter and once again see ourselves moving forward.

To get committed means we do not rely solely on feelings of passion and enthusiasm to propel us forward. Instead, we rely on a plan that will ensure that we are honoring our values and our commitments even when we are feeling reluctant. Having a clear plan and a set of values and goals helps us to hold ourselves accountable and make the choices we need to make in order to honor our commitments.

Getting committed requires that we stop being a victim to happenstance-that is, whatever happens to us that we believe keeps us from following through on our promises to ourselves and others. For example, you may want to get fit but complain that you have actually gained weight because you've attended many parties lately and couldn't help drinking and snacking too much. What happened to your commitment? Did you miss making the moment-to-moment choices you could've made that would have allowed you to meet your weight-loss goal? Perhaps you didn't have to say yes to all of the parties, or you could have chosen not to drink or snack at them. You could have chosen to eat only a portion of the meal, leaving the dessert and buttered bread on the table.

Or, perhaps one of your commitments you made to yourself was to write a book, but you complain that you have no time to do so. Perhaps you are missing the moment-to-moment opportunities to manage your time better and allowing other things in your life to take priority even though you value them less, such as maintaining a perfectly clean and organized house or keeping up on television programs.

Or, perhaps you want to create mutually loving relationships, but when you interact with others, you continue to say yes to others' needs and no to that whisper within that is telling you not to abandon yourself and your own commitments. When you finally recognize that your needs and feelings haven't been considered, you get angry and accuse everyone else of not caring for you when, in fact, it was you who did not stay committed to creating a mutual relationship by exercising your option to speak up in the moment as decisions were being made.

Holding yourself accountable includes noticing how you waste time or become distracted and avoiding making excuses such as "I don't have enough time" or "It's not my fault that this happened to me" to not meet your commitments. When we hold ourselves accountable to our commitments, we see the many choices before us and choose that which is in alignment with our commitment.

A woman was coming to me for coaching because she had a hard time staying focused on her priorities both in her personal life and at work. She called me just as she was supposed to be at our appointment to let me know that a contractor had come a day early and that she didn't know what to do. I could tell that she was feeling powerless as she told me what had happened and couldn't think of any choices in the moment but to let him in.

Looking to me for advice, she said, "I don't know what to do. I can't help it-he's still here. What would you do if you were me?" I spoke my truth and said, "It's up to you to decide what to do right now. But if it had been me, and I had made a commitment to someone else for an appointment and the contractor was early on his commitment, I would've asked him to come back at the committed time. Now, since you've let him in your home, it looks like you have a few choices: Miss your appointment with me and still pay me, or tell him now to go and come back later, and then get here as soon as you can. The choice is yours."

Within fifteen minutes, she was at my office, keeping her commitment and rediscovering her power to stick to her commitments. I could have let her off the hook, but I knew that this was her blind spot: She had a hard time seeing her choices and dealing with distractions along the way and often felt it was difficult to keep her commitments to others. The time we had together in our session was dedicated to helping her become more conscious of these choices and begin keeping her commitments so that she could feel good about herself.

Keeping commitments depends on the little daily choices we make. Let your daily choices reflect what you are choosing as a priority and commitment in your life.

WE WANT SO MUCH TO BE LOVED THAT OUR TENDENCY TO PEOPLE PLEASE CAUSES US TO VEER OFF COURSE AND GET ON OTHER PEOPLE'S AGENDA INSTEAD.

Recently, I was feeling incomplete in my life and, after further exploration, I realized that it was because I was not keeping my commitments to myself. My youngest had gone away to college and I had moved out to a house on a lake. For the first time in my life, I had a circle of single friends who were in the habit of spontaneously going out to the lake area restaurants, activities, and social gatherings where a lot of other single people congregate. After months of saying yes to many of these activities, I found myself feeling quite empty. It wasn't that I wasn't enjoying the company of the people I was with; it was that I was abandoning my commitments in the other areas of my life, including not taking enough time for exercise, writing, and quiet relaxation.

When I began to recognize the choices I was making were not in alignment with what was most important to me, at first I felt a bit like a victim of happenstance. I thought the problem was that I was giving in to others' needs more often than they were giving in to mine. I focused on how I was saying yes to their requests and accommodating them, and how often they were not accommodating my requests to get together at a time that was more workable for me. Then I realized that no one can take from me unless I allow them to do so, and that it was my tendency to accommodate that was keeping me from feeling complete.

With this new awareness, I began to get curious and wonder, "Why am I giving up the time I have allotted to things I say I am committed to, such as exercising, writing my book, and having quiet time? What am I attached to that is more important than those commitments?"

The answer was clear: I did not want to be alone, so I was saying yes to activities and invitations from others that were helping ensure that I wouldn't be by myself and would instead satisfy my need to feel loved.

As I thought about this tendency to say yes to others and to not choose to stay committed to what was most important to me, I realized that underneath that behavior choice was a lingering sense of low self-worth. It was an old wound beginning to ache again so that it could be further healed.

I began to wonder what would happen if I were to I stop abandoning my commitments, ask others for their support as I kept my commitments to myself, and remain in curiosity while I observed how they reacted to this change. What would I learn about the depth of my friendships?

This was a very freeing thought that allowed me to be more disciplined in sticking to my commitments and creating better boundaries with people. It allowed me to say yes to the lake activities with my friends when I really wanted to and to say no when I felt a need to keep the commitments in the other areas of my life so that I could stay balanced mentally, career-wise, spiritually, physically, and emotionally.

The way to stop people pleasing and accommodating is to become aware of the thoughts we hold as we are about to make our moment-to-moment choices. My thought was, "If I say *no* to them now, will they be there for me in the future when I need them?" Looking at my behavior, I could see that I was giving in order to get. Becoming honest with myself and realizing the real reason for my people pleasing made me see how manipulative I was actually being. By being honest about my thoughts, which were driving my behavior choices, I could consciously change my thoughts and begin a new course of action. The new thought I chose was, "Hmm . . . isn't that interesting... I wonder who will be there for me when I am available to socialize?"

Interestingly enough, as I was going through this awakening to an old people-pleasing pattern, my daughter, Alex, who was attending her first year at college, was facing similar issues. She had just gone off to the University of Wisconsin-Madison (a big ten college in Wisconsin, nicknamed "Mad Town") and was having a rough time the first few weeks in the dorm. She was struggling because she felt that the kids there didn't support her commitment to get enough sleep, treat her body well, study, and not think of "partying" as the only form of recreation. Later, as she realized their "partying" lifestyle just wasn't a fit for her, she was able to recommit to the type of activities she wanted to be involved in like dance, Bible study, and spending time with close friends. With this renewed focus and commitment, she was able to find the kind of people she wanted to spend time with, despite the obstacles, and keep her commitment to a healthy lifestyle.

Holding this new thought and being curious instead of judgmental helps us to create a feeling of high self-worth because we choose to honor our commitments and our relationship needs.

Being committed to someone or something means you actually carve out time in your schedule to focus on the thing or person you are committed to. If you believe that you are worth it, you will make loving choices for yourself instead of people pleasing. You will set boundaries with people so that you block out distractions and you trust that people will be there for you when you return. If they are not, you will be okay with that because you will realize that another person or a better opportunity is just right around the corner for you.

We can encourage others to support us by sharing with them what our commitments are. For example, you may have a new job and are feeling overwhelmed by this new commitment, needing more down time and sleep than you usually do. Instead of just saying no to someone's request to get together, you could tell them your situation and ask that they call you again in a few weeks, when you have adjusted to your change. It is not helpful to keep our commitments quiet and conjure up stories in our mind about how others will respond to us if we tell them we have other commitments in our lives besides our commitment to them.

To give up people pleasing, begin being honest with yourself as to why you are catering to their desires and not yours. Be open to their response when you share that you have other commitments, and trust that when they share their disappointment you won't feel the need to fight them or flee from your commitments. Trust that you will have the courage to allow the relationship to develop in its own way. If holding to your commitments means that the other person will not be there for you when you are available, trust that support will be available to you from someone else, and that it will show up in perfect timing. For example, you might be the first of your friends to get married and have a baby. Because of this new commitment in your life, you may not be as available to go out and socialize as you once did. Your friends, seeing that you have a new focus, may feel a loss and may not know how to support you in your new lifestyle. Allowing the relationship to unfold into a new form may mean that you will find support in another way, from parents you meet at a La Leche League meeting or a new moms' support group and so on.

As we stay committed to our goals and overcome obstacles, we allow life and relationships to unfold as they need to, letting go of our need to control and to our attachment to the form in which our goals are met.

Stop people pleasing. Begin to trust that support will come to you in perfect timing.

WHEN WE MAP OUT BUCKETS OF TIME IN OUR SCHEDULE, WE CAN GET COMMITTED.

Besides creating a mutually supportive environment, we need to become aware of our own time management style and how we sabotage ourselves from keeping our commitments and reaching our goals.

Often, we believe that we do not have enough time to reach our goals and keep our commitments when in fact the problem isn't a lack of time. Time is not a linear set of chunks: 60 minutes, 24 hours, 7 days a week, 365 days in the year, and so on. Time is a space in which we are given an opportunity to get clear, calm, confident, and committed to making choices that are in accord with our goals and values.

Achieving personal leadership requires us to perceive time and use it in a different way. Below are six different patterns of how we mishandle our time. When we see how we use or misuse time, we can work on changing our behavior pattern so that we can follow through on our commitments to ourselves instead of getting caught up in distractions and people pleasing.

- **Last-Minute Maggie.** Last-Minute Maggie procrastinates, and doesn't propel herself into action until she feels the burst of adrenaline that comes when she is up against a deadline and feeling anxious about meeting it. If you are a Last-Minute Maggie, notice that you depend on your anxiety to give you the impetus to act, and ask yourself, "How might I become more disciplined to choose to live up to my commitments in each moment as choices are presented to me instead of waiting until my needs are so urgent that I feel anxious?"

- **Creative Charlie.** Creative Charlie is full of so many creative ideas that he doesn't know which ones to choose. He makes many commitments to himself and others but isn't disciplined enough to follow through with any one of them. If you are a Creative Charlie, commit yourself to taking one idea and following through with it, making it come to fruition.

- **Juggling Joe.** Juggling Joe often has a hard time staying committed because he feels he must always say yes to life. He says yes to invitations from friends, yes to volunteer work, and yes to requests at work, and then wonders why he doesn't have enough time to meet his personal goals. If you are Juggling Joe, notice this tendency and develop the habit of saying to people, "Hmm . . . Let me think about it and get back to you." When you do think about the opportunity that has been offered to you, ask yourself, "Will saying yes bring me closer to my goals and help me keep my commitments?"

- **Perfect Pete.** Perfect Pete is disciplined to a fault. He goes to the extreme of making sure that everything he does is done perfectly. He is so focused on doing things perfectly, in the hope of being admired and not criticized, that he forgets that the purpose of getting committed is to feel complete within ourselves, not to control others' reactions to us. If you are Perfect Pete, it's important to regularly ask yourself, "Is perfection really needed here?"

- **Nurturing Nancy.** Having loving relationships is certainly important in our overall fulfillment and effectiveness in life. However, when we are too available to other people and become a Nurturing Nancy, it is because we have gone to the extreme of being more in tune with others' feelings and needs than we are with our own. In this case, we might be giving in order to get: We nurture others in the hope that we will receive nurturing from them. If you are Nurturing Nancy, ask yourself, "What would happen if I were to become more clear, calm, confident, and committed to my own life? Might I encourage others to do the same through my example?

- **Doubting Thomas.** Doubting Thomas is usually clear about his commitments but continually doubts whether or not he can achieve his goals. He wastes time waffling about the likelihood that he can have what he desires, and obsesses over every possible obstacle rather than just getting committed to making his dreams come true. If you are a Doubting Thomas, recognize that your problem is not a lack of time but a lack of commitment.

Knowing how we relate to time by wasting it, waiting until the last minute, making too many commitments, or spending valuable energy agonizing over whether or not our commitment is worth pursuing can cause us to veer off our course and break our commitments, especially in the face of an obstacle.

To take it a step further and reflect on why we choose these patterns of behavior verses investing more time in our commitments, we can ask ourselves the following provocative questions:

- Why do I need to feel anxious before I allow myself to attend to my own commitments?
- Why do I always feel the need to say *yes* to others and *no* to my commitments?
- What am I afraid will happen if I say *no*?

- Why don't I follow through with my creative ideas?
- Is fear holding me back?
- If so, what fear-the fear of disapproval? The fear of failure? The fear of abandonment?

After we have reflected on our patterns of mishandling time and commit ourselves to overcoming these tendencies, we can become proactive and organize our commitments into what I call buckets of time.

A bucket of time is space that you can fill with activities that fall into a particular category. For example, if you break down your time into the following categories, you can make a time bucket that creates the space needed to fulfill your commitments in that category. Here are some of the categories of activities we commit ourselves to:

- **Physical** (regular exercise, preparing and eating nutritious meals and snacks, getting health checkups, getting hair colored, etc.)

- **Spiritual** (attending church or temple, reading spiritual books, going on spiritual retreats, meditating, getting out in nature, etc.)

- **Intellectual** (reading the newspaper, reading quality books, having intellectual conversations, going back to school, etc.)

- **Relationships** (spending unstructured time with the people you love, engaging in activities you and the people you care about enjoy, planning birthday parties, helping your child with homework, etc.)

- **Vocational** (doing extra work to help you in your career, keeping up on reading new information in your field, attending conferences, getting extra training, etc.)

- **Practical** (cleaning your house, shopping, dealing with bills, yard work, doing car maintenance, etc.)

To determine how big your buckets of time need to be, under each category, list the commitments you are making to yourself or someone else that fall into that category. Try to indicate how long the activity will take and how often you want to engage in it. Your list might look something like this:

- **Physical**
  sleep eight hours every night
  work out for thirty minutes three times a week
  get a half-hour massage every other week
  color hair every four weeks (1 hr 30 minutes)
  schedule annual checkup at the doctor (2 hours)

- **Spiritual**
  spend half an hour a day in quiet relaxation
  attend church once a week (1 1/2 hours)
  read something spiritual every day
  give back through a philanthropic cause
  write a book

- **Intellectual**
  take a class
  read

- **Relational**
  spend time with loved ones: significant other, children, family, and friends

- **Vocational**
  work 40 hours a week
  entertain clients

- **Practical**
  clean the house
  do chores
  do errands
  pay bills

Organizing our commitments into buckets of time helps us to see what areas we are neglecting, and what areas we are spending too much time on. Below is an example of what a 49-year-old woman who attended one of my seminars came up with for her buckets of time. She was an entrepreneur, with two older children who lived on their own nearby. She was also a homeowner and was in a serious committed relationship. This is what her original list of buckets of time looked like:

- **Physical**

sleep eight hours a day	56 hours a week
work out 3 times a week	6 hours a week
nails every week	1.5 hours

- **Spiritual**

quiet time – 1/2 hour a day	3.5 hours
church once a week	1.5 hours
read something spiritual every day	7 hours a week
give back through a philanthropic cause	2 hours a week
write	10 hours a week
free time/"down time"	7 hours a week

- **Intellectual**

take a class	3 hours a week
read	4 hours a week

- **Relational**

spend time with loved ones:	
significant other	20 hours a week
children	5 hours a week
family	2 hours a week
friends	6 hours a week

- **Vocational**

work	40 hours a week
client event and entertainment	4 hours a week

- **Practical**

clean the house	3 hours a week
do chores	3 hours a week
do errands	2 hours a week
pay bills/financial management	1 hour a week

Add up your buckets of time = 187.5 hours in a week
The total amount of hours in a week = 168 hours in a week

Looking at this committed plan, you might observe some things that need adjusting. For example, if this were your schedule, you would have to make some choices so that you could effectively keep your commitments. In addition, you might wish to have some cushion time in your schedule, allowing for the unexpected. I usually recommend having at least 10 percent of your time allotted for this, which would equate to approximately 17 hours a week. In this case above, my client would have to eliminate 36.5 hours a week in order to create this cushion of time.

By noticing your time dilemmas, you can keep yourself from feeling frustrated and disappointed with yourself, as well as prevent yourself from feeling disappointed in and frustrated by others who don't live up to your expectations of how your schedule should unfold.

Looking at the example above, here are some possible adjustments this person could make:

- Combine the time spent with friends, family, and significant others by double dating, having dinner parties, etc.

- Combine exercise time with time spent with friends, family, and significant other.

- Combine the time spent on chores and errands with time spent enjoying the company of family members.

- Combine activities, such as: writing while doing laundry in the background; reading while doing the laundry etc.

- Download inspirational music onto your iPod so you can listen to it as you exercise or are paying bills.

- Eliminate an activity, for example, choosing not to take a class while engaged in the project of writing a book, so as not to get overloaded.

- Use technology to help you save time: pay bills online, use online banking, and so on.

- Hire help to do the laundry, chores, bill paying, etc., or delegate some of these activities to others (such as children).

Notice that the main point here is to be curious about where your time is going, to get clear by writing down how you're spending your time, and to calmly look at your options. When you create your buckets of time and think about altering them, you won't have to wait until situations get out of hand and people are putting pressure on you and expressing disappointment in you for not keeping your commitments. By using buckets of time, you can confidently make a commitment to the choices that honor what you want to create in your life, allowing you to feel complete because you are making conscious choices.

Remember: When you think that you don't have enough time for your commitments, it is because you are blind to how you are choosing to spend your time.
Map out your time commitments and you will be able to make clear and confident choices.

WE FEAR THAT GETTING COMMITTED AND FOLLOWING THROUGH ON OUR COMMITMENTS IS A SACRIFICE WHEN, IN FACT, IT GIVES US FREEDOM.

One of the biggest reasons we fear commitment is that we fear having to give up something we value in order to get what we want. Initially, when we pursue a goal-whether it's a business, relationship, or other type of goal-we will focus on the benefits of attaining that goal. But later, we start to think about what we will have to sacrifice if we continue pursuing it. For example:

- You started your own business so that you could have the freedom to make your own decisions and set your own schedule. Now you find yourself working long hours to make ends meet. You wonder, "Will this ever be worth it? Will I ever attain the financial freedom and time I was hoping to create for myself?" This thought could lead you to miss the opportunities right before your eyes.

- You joined a health club and went on a new eating regimen, and find yourself losing only a pound a week. You get discouraged and start wondering if you will ever lose the weight. Your thin friend orders a dessert at lunch and you are ready to give up your commitment and join her in the splurge.

- You are in a romantic relationship that is taking up a lot of your time. You are beginning to have some issues with your significant other and your friends are saying, "Don't put up with that. You can do better." You remember why you were first attracted to this person but now wonder if it is worth the effort to invest your heart, your time, and your energy in trying to understand your partner and resolve your differences. These thoughts create a wandering heart and eye and you stop feeling committed to the relationship.

- You have an employee who is not performing. You originally liked her enthusiasm, but now it seems that she puts little effort into her job. You don't know what to do except perhaps fire her. Instead of talking to her, putting her on a performance plan, and committing to helping her grow, you sit back and watch her fail and then hire someone new.

- Your child is struggling in school and is coming home with low grades on his report card. You don't like the choices he is making with his time and with his friends. You wanted him to go to the college you attended, but if he keeps it up, he will be lucky to get into any college at all. You are feeling frustrated and powerless and stop trying to help him in any way.

We often enter into commitments because we fantasize about the wonderful benefits we will receive: more security, safety, love, and belonging. But when we hit a hurdle that makes us believe our dream will not come true, we begin to focus on the sacrifices we must make of ourselves, our time, our money, and our heart. We begin to focus on what we are not getting instead of on what we are getting, and we lose our desire to stay committed.

Instead of focusing on what you are giving up, focus on the original reason you made the commitment and how you saw that commitment as a benefit. Remember, thoughts create feelings, feelings create behavior choices, and behavior choices create results. What you think about you bring about, so if you think about how you might overcome the obstacle that is causing you to want to abandon your original commitment, you will feel a renewed sense of energy that will keep you committed because you will be focusing on possibilities instead of feeling discouraged.

> *Stay committed by focusing on the vision, not the day-to-day benefits or sacrifices. This will help you persevere and give you freedom from continually reassessing your decisions.*

WHEN WE HANG AROUND WITH DOGS, WE CATCH FLEAS. WHEN WE SPEND TIME WITH OTHERS WHO CAN SUPPORT OUR COMMITMENTS, WE FIND IT EASIER TO FOLLOW THROUGH ON THOSE COMMITMENTS.

I am on the Board of Directors for Lad Lake, a nonprofit organization that supports youth at risk and their families. Recently, at one of our fundraisers, a young man who had been through the program spoke and shared his story. He talked about how he never knew his father and how his mother was a drug addict, unavailable to raise him properly. As a result of the lack of guidance and support in his life, he became involved in street gangs, getting into all kinds of trouble.

Then he found the Lad Lake organization, where he received the support and guidance he needed to finish his education and learn how to make good personal choices. When he got out of the program, he met up with his old friends again, who did not and could not support the new person he was. Eventually, because he was still struggling with a need to be loved, he found himself making poor choices again in order to feel a sense of belonging. This led to not one but two jail terms totaling eight years in prison. After he was released, he decided to go out of state to start over with new friends and to reconnect with some of the people he had met through the Lad Lake program so that he could get the support and the reinforcement he needed.

Now he is a contributing citizen, holding down a job and making good choices in his life. When he spoke in front of the group of 140 people at our fundraiser, he said, "I am proud that I am here today. I am proud of myself for the man that I have become. I have realized that in order to be my very best, I, like everyone else, need the support of others who believe in me..."

Although the details of this story may not fit your life, we can all relate to making choices that were not in our best interest at one time or another. If you believe you are so strong that someone else's bad choices will not affect you, think again. We are all vulnerable to others' influence, because we all have a strong need to be loved and to belong to a family or a group. If we do not have that natural support system, we will seek one out, whether our new support system encourages us to make good choices or bad ones. It's much easier to get committed when we acknowledge our need for support and actively seek out positive people who will support us when we make good choices.

Surround yourself with people who will support you in your commitments.

HIGHLY SUCCESSFUL PEOPLE STAY COMMITTED BECAUSE THEY DON'T FALL INTO THE PATTERN OF EXCUSE MAKING.

Have you ever noticed the differences between highly successful people and people who can't seem to achieve or maintain success? One of the biggest differences is that highly successful people see a situation or obstacle, remember their priorities and commitments, and choose accordingly. When they manifest what they want in their life, they feel good about themselves because they know they co-created their success with the help of God. Co-creation means that I listen within for the guidance I need to determine my direction and then I take action by assessing the possibilities before me, choosing my best options and persevering.

People who are excuse makers, on the other hand, see a situation and choose according to what they want in the moment or what is expected of them and then absolve themselves of the responsibility of making that choice by saying, "I couldn't help it," or "I really didn't want to do that, but I didn't have a choice." When they don't manifest what they want in the long run, they feel like a victim because they are blind to what they could have done differently in their moment-to-moment choices to create a different outcome.

Excuse making comes from our tendency to become fearful under pressure instead of becoming curious about how we can keep our commitments in a difficult situation when it arises. When we are clear about our commitments and why we have made them, and we stay calm under pressure, we confidently make the choice that will help us stay on the course of our commitments. Excuse makers fall prey to the instant gratification of safety, security, love, and belonging instead of staying focused on what their commitments are.

I often hear excuse making in the workplace when someone does not speak up in front of his or her boss. Say, for example, that I am working with a manager of a department and he aspires to be a vice president. When I am observing him interacting with the boss, I will often notice that the manager is not speaking the same truth that he shared with me when I met with him alone. Instead, he loses his voice or agrees with the boss even when that isn't how he really feels.

When I get together again with the manager and point out what I observed in his conversation with his boss, the manager will often start making excuses, saying things like:

- I wanted to speak up but I couldn't-he kept interrupting me!
- I don't agree with him on what we are doing but he is so busy, I never get a chance to tell him how I feel.
- Whenever I do speak up, he disagrees with me, so it doesn't do any good anyway.
- Even when I try to talk to him outside of a meeting, he is always on his cell phone or has his door shut.

A person who is not an excuse maker and is committed to becoming the best leader he can be would notice these situations and ask himself, "How might I get my viewpoint across to my boss in a way that he can hear me?" On the other hand, if he were an excuse maker and secretly had the need to please, he might try to manipulate his boss into promoting him by becoming a yes man instead of asserting himself, or he might make up all kinds of excuses to avoid a potential conflict.

Again, what we think about, we bring about. Instead of trying to manipulate the outcomes of your life and making up excuses along the way, notice your thoughts. Change them to open and trusting thoughts, and you will find ways to keep your commitment to being your best self.

Another common excuse I hear as I coach businesses and individuals, and even when I'm talking with friends, is: "I'm sorry I didn't (call you back, remember your birthday, get you that information on time as I promised). I was busy." This is an excuse we all seem to accept rather than looking at the truth, which is that we all have choices. Successful people who keep their commitments don't use "I am busy" as an excuse, nor do they accept it. That's not to say successful people don't forget someone's birthday or don't call someone back right away-they are human too. The difference is that they don't make excuses and will be honest and say, "I forgot, I guess I am a bit overwhelmed these days" or "I have over committed myself," or "I had other commitments I had to attend to first." The point here is that the language they use is more clear, calm, and confident instead of foggy, anxious, and powerless.

If you are to practice the sixth piece of the personal leadership puzzle, you must stop using busy-ness as your excuse to not meet your commitments.

If you want to be committed, focus on what you can do instead of what you can't do.
Give up excuse making and ask yourself, "How might I...?"

SEVENTH PIECE:

GET COMMUNICATING!
CALL THE BIRD OUT OF THE BUSH

To get communicating, the seventh piece of the personal leadership puzzle, we need to become aware of our thoughts, needs, feelings, and dreams, and openly and directly communicate them to others. When we communicate effectively, we are no longer hiding who we really are. By sharing our true self with others, we are honoring our true self.

As we commit to personal leadership, we realize that communicating is a necessary piece in leading a complete life, because as we build and sustain the life we want for ourselves, we need to be able to articulate our likes, dislikes, needs, thoughts, ideas, and desires with others and speak up even when it feels uncomfortable to do so. If we do not speak up, we will lose our power and we will not feel complete. Keeping our connection with our confidence and courage is an important part of communicating, especially when we imagine an undesirable outcome like being dismissed, offending someone, or making someone angry.

When we "get communicating," we invite others to do the same, which in turn helps us to discover what level of interpersonal rapport the relationship can tolerate. In some cases, relationships can only tolerate the exchange of facts, while others can go deeper into exchanging thoughts, ideas, and dreams, and others can go as deep as exploring and sharing inner feelings and experiences with one another. The only way to know how much intimacy a relationship can bear is to communicate.

To effectively communicate with others, we need to be aware of the communication that goes on within us. This is called intrapersonal communication, the art of understanding and managing our own inner dialogue before we speak to others. Subtle feelings and thoughts that we are not conscious of, if shared, can lead to destructive, unproductive, and confusing communication with others. When it comes to personal leadership, we "get communicating" with ourselves first. We listen to the still small voice inside that wants to lead us and guide us; we pay attention to our feelings and thoughts; and we work at understanding our heart's calling, which clues us in to knowing what is most important to us. Good intrapersonal communication requires that we become clear about our thoughts and feelings before we articulate them so that we say what we mean and mean what we say.

TO GET COMMUNICATING, WE NEED TO BE INTUITIVE AND LOOK FOR THE HIDDEN MESSAGES IN NONVERBAL COMMUNICATION.

A company asked me to come in and do some sales coaching with an account manager who was having trouble with a new client. Normally, the company provided full service to their clients, but in this case, the client wanted some of the work to be done by a contractor that he had worked with previously.

When the client announced that he wanted to use this private contractor, it changed the scope of the account manager's job. She felt threatened. As the outside contractor took over an aspect of the work and began to make decisions without clearing them through the account manager, she started feeling even more threatened. She felt she should be calling the shots because initially she had been in charge of seeing that the entire project was done properly, and now she was feeling scared that the contractor's creativity was going to put the project over budget. The account manager began to react out of her unconscious fear and began to try to regain full control of the project by trying to prove herself, insisting to the client that she and her company should once again be in charge of all aspects of the project. When her request was rejected, she stopped speaking up and became more anxious.

After learning the history of the account relationship and hearing the account manager tell me about her struggle to prove herself and be in control of the situation, I approached her and said, "It appears to me the problem is not how the outside contractor is acting, but how you are reacting to the contractor. It appears to me that you're reacting out of fear. Is that true?"

After I called the bird out of the bush, a term I use in coaching to address the hidden feelings and behaviors going on that the client is unaware of, she went on to tell me about how she was afraid that if she didn't take control over every aspect of the project, the project's schedule would slip and it would go over budget, and she would then end up losing the account altogether. After she admitted to feeling afraid, I could sense how great her fear was and explored it further, asking, "What is all that fear about for you?"

It only took this one question to bring to the surface her emotions, and she burst into tears. "Oh, we are getting at the core now," she said. "This account feels so familiar."

"Tell me more about that," I probed. She told me a story about how a similar situation had happened to her just one year previously and how she had lost the deal completely. After hearing the details of her story, I said, "I can understand why you are scared. It sounds like the exact same type of situation. The only difference is that now you have experience and hindsight that can be applied to this new situation. What do you think it was that you were supposed to learn during that earlier experience that your wiser, more caring, and more empowered self can now bring to this client?"

She was still blocked and had no idea, so I probed further. "Why do you think that the other client ended up going to another company? What did they think they could get from another company that they couldn't get from you?" She proceeded to tell me about a special service that they had wanted but that her firm had decided not to provide given the limited budget the client had. "I told them that since they couldn't get as much financing as they wanted, they couldn't have that service. I was afraid if they couldn't accept that decision, we might lose the entire deal because we had already gone over budget and were beyond the point that we could sacrifice any more financially in order to meet their expectations."

Hearing this fear pop up once again revealed her tendency to ignore the bird in the bush or kill the deal because she was so afraid. Knowing this, I asked, "Do you think that perhaps if you had probed further to explore their most important priorities and their feelings about this issue that you could have eventually gotten them to discover the truth themselves-that they were going to have to sacrifice some of their wishes to get what they really needed with the limited budget they had? Can you see how forcing this truth on them before they were ready to accept it, by simply insisting that they couldn't have what they wanted, could have cost you the deal?"

She laughed and said, "Probably so. It's funny. They went with the other company and what they ended up with didn't include the service they were demanding anyway." As she realized this truth, she began to cry again. "It's okay," I told her. "It's time to let it go. You've learned something valuable. Now you know that deeper listening and being honest about your fears, and theirs, pays off. Perhaps what you have to do in this situation is call your bird out of the bush, and call their bird out of the bush. Right?"

Her boss, whom I had been helping with leadership development, was sitting in on the meeting and complimented me afterward. He told me, "I would never have thought that her problem was fear-based. I kept on thinking about getting her to strategize a new approach, not about getting to the root cause behind her approach like you did. How did you know that fear was at the heart of her struggle with this account?"

I shared with him the process that I used in coaching so that he could use it in other situations in the future. I call this process the Intuitive Coaching Theory, and it involves observing one's behavior (calling the bird out of the bush) and probing to discover our hidden thoughts and beliefs that are incongruent with what we say we want in order to expose our fear-based attachments. Once the fear-based attachments are discovered, we can consciously choose a new thought pattern and belief and bring about the results we desire. In this case, the account manager had a fear-based attachment to making the sale. The client had picked up on her anxiety about the sale and lacked confidence in the account manager's ability to deliver the part of the project that ended up being contracted out. He felt more comfortable going with a contractor he had used before. By using the Intuitive Coaching Theory, I helped the account manager to recognize the conflict between what she said she wanted (delivering the entire package to the client, within budget) and what her hidden thoughts and beliefs were (that she couldn't do so).

I explained to the owner of the company that I developed the Intuitive Coaching Theory after testing it on thousands of clients over my 20 years in my personal and business development business, and that it was based on four communication and psychology theories:

1) **Cognitive dissonance** (a theory created by psychologist Leon Festinger in 1956): Uncomfortable tension results when we hold two conflicting thoughts at the same time, or when our thoughts and beliefs do not match our actions.

2) **Behaviorist theory** (a theory created by John B. Watson and B. F. Skinner): All behavior is the result of habits that have been learned; these habits can also be unlearned and replaced by new, more acceptable ones by implementing an effective reward and consequence program. Watson believed that we should focus on overt behavior that can be observed rather than speculating about subconscious motives or hidden thinking processes.

3) **The Johari window** (a theory created by Joseph Luft and Harry Ingham):

	Known to Self	Not Known to Self
Known to Others	1 **OPEN**	2 **BLIND**
Not Known to Others	3 **HIDDEN**	4 **UKNOWN**

The Johari window is a four-paned "window" that divides personal awareness into four different types, each represented by a quadrant: open, hidden, blind, and unknown.

Each person has a Johari window. Here's a description of my window:

1. The "open" quadrant includes the things about myself that I, as well as you, are aware of-facts, behaviors, dreams, needs, preferences, and motives. Because you are reading my book, you know my name and that I am a coach for businesses and individuals. You know that I want to help people create a complete life for themselves.

2. The "blind" quadrant includes the things about me that you are aware of but I am not aware of. So, for example, I could be tapping my foot unconsciously, but you might notice my behavior. You could call the bird out of the bush and point out my behavior, and ask if I'm nervous or if I just have a lot of physical energy today. When people are concerned about learning and self-development, they are more likely to allow people to reflect their behaviors to them and explore what is behind those behaviors.

3. The "hidden" quadrant includes the things about myself that I'm aware of that you are not aware of. You may not know that I was married three times. I may choose to wait to discuss this with you until I have built trust, or until I feel that my sharing this information would be for a higher purpose. If I do tell you things about myself that you're unaware of, I am choosing to engage in self-disclosure.

4. The "unknown" quadrant includes the things that I do not know about myself and you, too, do not know about me. For example, I may disclose a feeling that I had in a new relationship, and as we both attempt to understand its significance, we might both become aware of what my feelings and thoughts are regarding this relationship.

4) Maslow's Hierarchy of Needs (a theory created by Abraham Maslow in 1943): We strive first to meet our most basic needs and then we strive to meet needs that are higher up in the hierarchy of human needs.

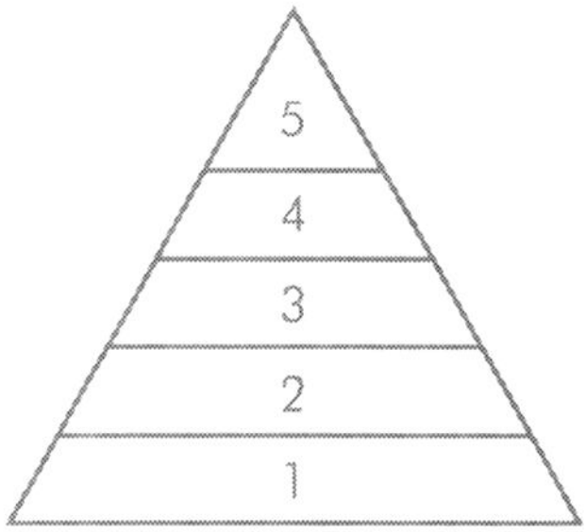

Diagram of Maslow's hierarchy of needs.
5. Actualization
4. Status (esteem)
3. Love/belonging
2. Safety
1. Physiological (biological needs)

According to Maslow's hierarchy of needs, we only begin to think about the highest levels of needs when the needs on the lower levels have been met. The more growth we do, the more we recognize our higher levels of needs. So, for instance, if I am focused on my basic survival needs for food, clothing, and shelter, I can't recognize my need for safety, much less my need for a sense of belonging, love, esteem, or actualization.

All four of these theories fit into how my Intuitive Coaching Theory works:

Imagine that our...

- Thoughts create feelings
- Feelings create the behavior choices we make
- Behavior choices create results

If you are not getting the results you want, at work or at home:

First, notice the results you are getting and the gap between what is and what it is you say you want.

Second, notice your behavior and the behavior of the person you are interacting with. What are you doing? What is he doing? What are you saying? What is he saying? How are you acting? How is he acting?

Third, notice the emotional energy that you or the other person is operating from. Are you coming from fear or from love? Which of these emotions is he coming from?

Fourth, imagine the thoughts that would create that kind of emotional energy. What might the belief or thought be?

Fifth, once you discover the fear-based limited thinking, replace it with a new way of seeing things.

Work the process backward. First, just observe the situation and notice how the results are different from what the person says he wants (cognitive dissonance). Then, observe the behaviors. Ask yourself if these behaviors are rooted in fear (perhaps a fear of not getting one's needs met) or rooted in love and concern for each others' needs (behavioral theory). From here, you can get to the root cause of the behavior by imagining the hidden thought process and belief system that is operating and determining that person's choice of behavior, unbeknownst to him (the Johari window). When you do that, you can ask yourself, "Hmm . . . isn't that interesting? I wonder . . . what is the attachment to (safety, security, love, and belonging) that this person has?" (Notice that safety, security, love, and belonging are all needs identified in Maslow's hierarchy of needs).

When we are focused on "What's in it for me?" we are engaging in fear-based thinking, feeling, and behaving, which clients, friends, and family can feel and recognize at some level. On the other hand, when we are focused on, "How might we get you what is most important to *you*?" we inspire others to trust us and want to choose to be with us and work with us. Whatever our focus is, we communicate it to others; if not verbally, then nonverbally. To get communicating, we have to be clear on what our focus is and use the five-step approach of the Intuitive Coaching Theory.

Practice looking behind the behavior to the heart of the matter so that you can get communicating.

TO GET COMMUNICATING, WE NEED TO CALL THE BIRD OUT OF THE BUSH. THE PROBLEM IS WE OFTEN KILL OR IGNORE THE SQUAWKING BIRD, INSTEAD OF CALLING IT OUT TO DISCOVER WHAT IT HAS TO TELL US.

When we practice the discipline of intrapersonal communication, we realize that becoming aware of what is happening inside of us and keeping our focus on our inner feelings and thoughts takes work. We recognize that when we stop checking in with ourselves, those feelings and thoughts will come to the surface anyway and we'll unconsciously express them through our body language, our behavior choices, our tone of voice, and our emotional mood. In fact, 90 percent of our communication is this type of more subtle, nonverbal communication. It's as if our hidden feelings and thoughts are a bird hiding in a bush, rustling around, trying to get our attention and the attention of others.

Others who are more conscious and aware than we are in the moment will notice that we are sending out subtle signals about what we are thinking and feeling, even though we are not fully aware of them. They might choose to "call the bird out of the bush," acknowledging that we are subtly communicating a lost part of ourselves that we have not listened to and fully embraced. It may be the part of ourselves that is scared or hurt, or the part of ourselves that believes we are not "enough." If we are open to communicating, we will consider this reflection of ourselves and wake up to what we are thinking and feeling. If we are not open to communicating, we will become defensive and try to fight or flee rather than do the difficult work of exploring our deepest thoughts and beliefs.

Learning to call the bird out of the bush and share our observations with others is an art, but unfortunately, until it is developed, we often ignore the bird in the bush, or kill it. We flee from the conversation that needs to happen and ignore what we are noticing, or we speak up before we have become aware of our deeper feelings and thoughts, reacting to the bird in the bush because we have not fully embraced our own fear or judgment. When two unconscious people are communicating with their own hidden birds in the bush, the communication becomes defensive and can quickly become destructive.

When we ignore the bird in the bush and claim we didn't even know it was there, we do so because we have rationalized away our gut feelings and needs. We tell ourselves, "It must be my imagination," or "I shouldn't let that bother me." Unfortunately, if we ignore the bird in the bush often enough, we get into the habit of ignoring our inner voice that is asking us to acknowledge our deepest feelings and beliefs as well as our needs and perceptions. When we live with this kind of denial, we do not "get communicating" with ourselves or with others. Instead of calling the bird out of the bush and speaking up, we may become depressed, angry, or anxious. However, if we get communicating with ourselves, we can explore our feelings and thoughts without judgment and then be able to do the same with others.

When we ignore the bird in the bush long enough and the bird keeps squawking, we may eventually decide we've had enough. Then we are likely to want to kill the bird in the bush because its squawking has grown extremely irritating to us. Killing our own bird in the bush can be done with any self-destructive behavior, such as drinking too much, losing our temper, or even cutting our wrists-anything that will continue to numb us from hearing what is going on inside of us. When it's someone else's bird in the bush and we've had enough of it, we can potentially become abusive to them physically, emotionally, and verbally, trying desperately to quiet their squawking bird so we do not have to deal with ours. When we have gone to the extreme of wanting to kill the bird in the bush, whether that is ours or theirs, it is because we are out of control emotionally and have lost our ability to communicate with ourselves and others. If only we would have called the bird out of the bush right away, while emotions were still manageable, we could have started to communicate and potentially gotten the bird to quiet down.

Being afraid of confrontation is one of the biggest reasons we ignore the bird in the bush when we are communicating with other people. We may hear it squawking as the other person begins to sound defensive or angry, or shuts down and refuses to talk about a particular subject. Fearing that a confrontation will result in their fighting their own bird in the bush by fighting with us, we will often choose to ignore the squawking just as they are choosing to do. When we do this, problems and conflicts do not get resolved, needs do not get met, and we feel angry, anxious, or sad, because on some level, we believe there is no hope for a greater connection and better communication with the other person.

We hear the squawking of the bird in the bush in many situations:

- A child is acting up to get your attention and displaying undesirable behaviors such as sassing you, rolling her eyes, or disobeying you. Or, you are gossiping or being dishonest with others behind their back.

- A client is showing signs of disinterest and not returning your calls. Or, you are making yourself unavailable for a conversation with someone who needs to speak to you.

- Someone is continuing to give you excuses for not meeting his deadlines and commitments. Or, you are making excuses for your own lack of follow through.

- Someone is saying one thing but behaving in another way. Or, your beliefs and your behavior are out-of-sync with each other.

It's important to get communicating and call the bird out of the bush any time we are experiencing something that is drawing our attention but is not being communicated in words, or when the words don't match up with the nonverbal communication. When we call the bird out of the bush, we begin to put words to the unconscious behavior we see in others and ourselves, and create greater awareness, understanding, and connection for everyone.

However, knowing how to effectively call the bird out of the bush is important. We have all been in an unproductive conversation that has sounded something like this, "You seem awfully angry lately." "No I'm not!" "Then why are you always snapping at everyone?" "I'm not snapping at everyone, you're just sensitive!" "No, I think you are taking your frustration at work out on us!" This could go on and on.

This dynamic is not calling the bird out of the bush. It is a blame and shame game that keeps ping-ponging back and forth and doesn't lead anywhere but to hurt feelings and defensiveness. Calling the bird out of the bush would sound different. It would sound something like, "I noticed that lately you have seemed more agitated than usual, is something bothering you?" If the person attacked you back right away because they didn't want to deal with their bird in the bush, and said, "No! That's your imagination. You're just sensitive!", you would notice that and stay connected with yourself, instead of trying to force your perspective on them. You would feel any hurt, self-doubt, or anger that was a result of their angry response. By staying with your own bird in the bush and simply calling theirs out without killing it, you could perhaps come back to the conversation later, when the other person has had a chance to think about your question and do some personal reflection.

I observed this dynamic when coaching a couple that was in a somewhat new relationship. Both of them deeply desired to break out of the traditional roles they had played in the past with their previous partners. They realized that to maintain an authentic emotional connection, they would have to communicate in a different way to one another and learn to call the bird out of the bush whenever one or both of them was not consciously seeking his or her own truth or that of the other.

As I spoke with both of them alone and together, I shared a five-step communication process that helps us to call the bird out of the bush, especially when we are working with a partner who is unwilling to "get communicating."

The *five steps to calling the bird out of the bush* are:

1. Share your observations.
2. Share your feelings about those observations.
3. Be curious about what is behind the behavior in the bush.
4. State what changes you would like to see.
5. Ask, "How might we create a situation that is workable for both of us?"

They found this five-step process helpful to use as they communicated about things they had said to one another and behaviors they had exhibited that did not fit with what they said they wanted to create. Although both claimed that they did not want to fall into the patterns of their previous relationships, they found themselves doing so. One of the patterns that showed up was the man not being clear and honest about what he wanted and instead, withdrawing emotionally at times. Because her last husband had done this, over the years she had learned how to deny her own feelings of abandonment, eventually getting fed up with the emotional disconnection. When this happened in her new relationship, both she and her new husband wanted to ignore the bird in the bush at first, but eventually, she wanted to kill it (she would start screaming at him, telling him she'd had it!).

To help them get communicating and call the bird out of the bush, I shared with them the process they would use if they went ahead and ignored or killed the bird. I told them that *ignoring the bird* would look like this:

1. You notice that something is bugging you.
2. Your feelings are intense and you get scared.
3. You tell yourself it's not worth discussing because nothing would change anyway or you may say something you'll regret. Or, perhaps you convince yourself the other person can't handle the truth.
4. You don't say anything and do not speak your truth.
5. Eventually, you become disconnected from yourself and the relationship, get overly anxious, or get depressed.

As I laid out these steps, the woman nodded her head and said, "Yep, that sounds like what I have done in the past-ignored the subtle, withdrawing bird in the bush and then, eventually, I wanted to leap after that bird and let him have it!"

"Good," I said. "Recognizing your patterns is a big step out of your past and the first step in transforming into a new way of operating. Now let's talk about another pattern that could occur if you don't get communicating."

I told the woman and her husband that when we quickly react to the bird in the bush, we can overlook the importance of taking time for intrapersonal communication. Listening to our inner dialog allows us to be aware of our thoughts and feelings before we speak to the other person, so that we express what we really think and feel in our heart instead of saying one thing but giving them a totally different message with our nonverbal communication.

Quickly reacting and *killing the bird in the bush* would look like:

1. You notice that something is bugging you.
2. You have feelings about it but don't fully understand them; you just know they are intense.
3. You don't go deeper into understanding your feelings so that you can express them. Instead, you let the other person experience your feelings about it and lash out because you don't want to deal with your feelings.
4. You don't let the other person say very much before you interrupt to express your intense feelings.
5. You start to build resentment toward that other person or you end up very anxious, depressed, or angry.

As I shared this with the couple, they both laughed. "Ahhh . . . I can relate!" he humbly admitted.

"So can I," she said.

"That is why I often withdraw into the bush and deny what is happening. I am afraid that I might come across too harsh if I speak up right away. I've done that before and I guess I'm now going to the other extreme."

I went on to say that calling the bird out of the bush, using this five-step communication process, is very helpful in the beginning stages of professional and personal relationships, because it reveals to us how approachable that person can be and how conscious he or she is willing to become.

I practice this technique when I help companies interview potential employees. In one particular interview, I remember noticing some inconsistencies on the interviewee's resume and began to question these discrepancies in detail. When I did, he grew increasingly annoyed with my observations and concerns. Noticing his irritation when I questioned him, I asked, "Did you have an issue with anger at any of your jobs?" He admitted to struggling with anger at a job in which he was fired because of the way he treated other employees in other departments. When I asked why he was being let go of his current job, he said, "Downsizing."

This didn't ring true for me, since he had told me that the company had let go of two of the five people and he was one of the two let go, and yet he claimed he had been the company's top performer. I called the bird out of the bush and told him about my hunch, asked for specific names and numbers from his last job, and told him I would be checking out his references, specifically asking about his temperament. As I shared with him what I had observed, how I felt, and what I needed to soothe my curiosity, his temper flared. Calling the bird out of the bush was all it took for me to trust my gut that my hunches were correct.

Calling the bird out of the bush can also help us to make wiser choices in our friendships and romantic partners. Looking back at my failed relationships, I see a common pattern that I contributed to the dynamic: I would not address issues I saw and would ignore the bird in the bush during the infatuation stage. Then, later, I would try to talk about the stuff that was bothering me, only to find out that the person I was already becoming attached to didn't want to communicate that deeply or honestly and simply wanted to resolve issues quickly or ignore them.

When I did start to call the bird out of the bush, my inquiries and observations were met with defensiveness and resistance and that would inhibit emotional intimacy between us. Not knowing how to deal with it at the time, I did what most people would do when they get sick of ignoring the bird in the bush: I would turn up the volume and start attacking the bird!

Well, of course, my increased volume and more critical tone of voice got my partner's attention, but eventually it led to killing the bird in the bush-and the relationship. In hindsight, it would have been wise for both of us to call the bird out of the bush earlier in the relationship so that we could both have seen whether the relationship could tolerate the level of emotional intimacy and honesty that we desired. If it couldn't, I would've had the opportunity to be with my own hidden bird in the bush-my sadness and disappointment-so that I could eventually grieve the loss of a potential relationship and move on, knowing something better was in store for me. But because being with my disappointment and sadness was difficult for me, and was my lost bird in the bush, I ignored it. The lessons we learn when we are afraid to face our own feelings and those of others!

Risk calling the bird out of the bush early on in the relationship. It allows you to have an effective dialog with yourself as well as to share with someone else your observations, feelings, and curiosity about his or her behavior. When you call the bird out of the bush, you can get communicating.

TO GET COMMUNICATING EFFECTIVELY, YOU NEED TO BE OPEN AND TRUSTING, ALLOWING MATTERS TO UNFOLD IN PERFECT TIMING, INSTEAD OF OPERATING OUT OF FEAR-BASED THINKING.

To discern whether we (or someone else) are operating out of fear-based thinking or love-based thinking, we can observe the following two patterns:

Pattern #1: We (or someone else) are focused on:
What's in it for me? Make me feel important!

This is fear-based thinking, and is predicated on:

- ***Fear*** and attachment to the outcome
- ***Judgment*** that we might not get what we want because of some story we have told ourselves in our head
- ***Control*** that causes us to try to maneuver, manipulate, and force things to get what we want

Pattern #2: We are focused on:
What's in it for you? Let me make you feel important!

This is love-based thinking, and is predicated on:

- ***Open***, authentic, and collaborative communication
- ***Trusting*** that the communication process will help the conversation unfold and reveal the truth regarding what the relationship can sustain
- ***Allowing*** the outcome to unfold as it needs to in

perfect timing, trusting that this situation or another one will provide for your needs

Which of these two communication patterns we engage in is determined by our ability to recognize our tendency to be attached to our own agenda and the outcome. As Maslow's hierarchy of needs indicates, we all have needs and are in process of the development of our true self. However, our tendency is to believe that we are not "enough" and therefore, we feel, we must worry about our basic needs being met. This fear causes us to act out of Pattern #1.

A Pattern #1, fear-based reaction may include situations such as:

- *You are in sales* and want to convince a client to order a certain product by the end of the month so that you make your quota. This is in contrast to probing to find out their needs and goals and then being open and collaborative with them in finding a viable solution that will meet their immediate and long-term goals, trusting that you will meet your quota one way or another.

- *You are a leader at your company* and want an employee to stop doing what he is doing so he can assist you on a project that is critical to your list of goals for the day. This is in contrast to having an open conversation with him about his priorities and collaborating with him on a decision that best meets the company's goals and priorities.

- *You are a parent* and see that your child is spending a lot of time with what you believe is an undesirable friend. You want him to end the friendship because you are afraid of what might happen and insist that your child can no longer associate with that person. This is in contrast to having an open conversation with your child and seeking to understand what he gets from that relationship, expressing why you are concerned, and exploring with your child what he might do given your feelings and perceptions.

- *You are in a romantic relationship* with someone who does not like to spend as much time with you as you like to spend with him. You start making arrangements to get together more often and you try to entice the other person into joining you. This is in contrast to having an open and honest conversation about what expectations each of you has, so that together, you can create a mutually satisfying relationship.

Notice that in the above situations, you might be feeling fear inside, but the key is to bear witness to that fear and own up to it so that you can engage in an open, collaborative conversation that will lead to truth and to the highest good of the all.

Although sometimes being open can make us feel vulnerable, being truthful and knowing the truth will set us free from all the frustration we would feel if we were carrying fear in our heart and judgment in our mind and struggling to control the outcome.

Choose to let go of fear, judgment, and control. This will allow you to communicate in an open and trusting manner.

"ASK-LEADING" ENSURES THAT WE HAVE MADE A CONNECTION.

To communicate effectively and connect at a deeper level with someone when we are calling the bird out of the bush, we can use a technique called "Ask-leading." When we observe something that is getting our attention, like a bird squawking in a bush, we can share what we are noticing, share what we are experiencing and feeling, and respectfully lead them to their own discovery by asking, "What is that about for you?"

Asking the question "What is that about for you?" honors other people's self-discovery process and invites them to acknowledge and own the hidden part of themselves that they have been avoiding because being aware of it makes them feel uncomfortable or even causes them pain. None of us wants to experience difficult emotions such as fear, unworthiness, anger, or sadness, but even when we try to repress them, we end up communicating them anyway. The question "What is that about for you?" comes from love and encourages the other person to set aside his fear and explore how he genuinely feels. I call this "Ask-leading" because the question you ask leads the other person into self-exploration.

When using the Ask-leading technique, it is crucial to put aside any tendency to judge because when your invitation comes with a curious observation, not a judgmental one, you create a safe place for people to look at themselves. But when you observe with judgment, the receiver of your message will know he is not safe, because no matter what you say, his intuition will cause him to pick up on the 90 percent of your communication that tells him you are sitting in judgment of him-he'll receive the messages that you send out through your body language, your tone of voice, and your emotional energy. In fact, if you are being judgmental, that means you have a fear of some kind that you are not aware of, and you need to acknowledge that fear, own it, and explore it.

To use the Ask-leading technique effectively for your own self-discovery, check in with yourself and ask, "Why do I feel a need to be judgmental as I call the bird out of the bush? Am I afraid something will happen if the bird is not called out of the bush? What is that fear about for me?"

As you use the Ask-leading technique, be aware of your intention. Are you trying to foster your own self-development as well as someone else's by raising your level of awareness and helping him to do so as well?

Ask-leading can be used at work and at home, in the following ways:

- *Your teenager is acting moody:* You can call the bird out of the bush and Ask-lead the conversation by saying, "I've noticed that you have been more sad and short-tempered lately. What is that about for you?"

- *Your significant other is distant:* You can call the bird out of the bush and Ask-lead the conversation by saying, "I've noticed that you seem far away from me lately. What is that about for you?"

- *Your coworker is not handing in her projects on time:* You can call the bird out of the bush and Ask-lead the conversation by saying, "I've noticed that you haven't been meeting your deadlines lately. What is that about for you?"

- *Your boss has been more critical toward you:* You can call the bird out of the bush and Ask-lead the conversation by saying, "I've noticed that you have not been happy with my performance lately. What is that about for you?"

When we Ask-lead someone to share what is hidden to us and to him, he will often initially react by denying the truth. If he does, don't take it personally! It is not about you, it is about him: He has a hidden aspect of himself that he is not sure he wants to look at or share with you. If this should happen, be respectful of his personal and emotional boundary of self-disclosure. Just observe his reaction and stay connected to your own center and your own truth by saying to yourself, "Hmm...isn't that interesting? He is not willing to look at that aspect of himself yet or discuss it with me. I wonder what that is about for him?" By staying with your curiosity, you keep yourself from becoming fearful, from judging the other person or the process, and from trying to control the timing of when the other person will allow himself to become aware.

Stay curious and use Ask-leading to foster communication. It will bring you to the truth-your own, and others'.

IF YOU CAN BEAR WITNESS TO YOUR "REACTOR WITHIN," YOU CAN HAVE A BETTER COMMUNICATION-CONNECTION.

The balance between effective communication and emotional intimacy is hard to master unless we have become aware of our own "reactor within." I call this the "reactor within" because the pressures we feel and the demands we place on a relationship often get in the way of our ability to effectively communicate and create a healthy emotional intimacy with someone. This is because we do not fully recognize and acknowledge our needs and feelings and we fear that they will not be met. Within each of us is a strong "reactor" that demands that we experience four things:

1) Feeling important
2) Feeling loved (the reactor within asks, "What about me?")
3) Being right
4) Staying connected or maintaining our autonomy (I refer to this as "the urge to merge" or the "need to navigate" so as to keep separate)

I saw these four demands affecting the relationship of a couple I was recently coaching. They had been married for over 20 years and were now separated, trying to figure out what went wrong. They had two children, two dogs, a close extended family, a beautiful house, and their health, but there was no emotional intimacy in their marriage. Once they called the bird out of the bush on their relationship and admitted to themselves and each other that there was little connection left between them, we could begin communicating.

Instead of ignoring the reactor within that each of them had, we made a list of what each reactor within needed. This helped each of them to be more conscious and aware so that they could share their needs with one another by using healthy communication. The list consisted of what each one of them needed to feel important, considered, validated, and connected yet autonomous. When each of them openly and honestly disclosed their authentic self, they could release their fear that their needs would not be met, as well as their beliefs that their needs would be judged and that they would have to control each other to get their needs met. Now they were able to recognize that openly communicating and trusting each other would allow the relationship to form and grow.

Through sessions that led to more self-awareness and self-disclosure, each of them could bear witness to his or her own reactor within and to that of the other with more compassion. This was possible because they could see how similar they really were, even when their reactor's behavior looked a bit different from the other's. Understanding that each of them had the need to feel important, considered, validated, connected, and autonomous, they could engage in an open conversation that would lead to better communication.

As the couple began to experience authentic communication, they were able to change the unhealthy, fear-based dynamic between them and create one that was based on greater emotional intimacy.

The new communication dynamic was based on the needs of communication and emotional intimacy, which are in contrast to the needs of the reactor within:

<u>The four things a reactor demands:</u>

1) Our reactor wants to feel important.

2) Our reactor questions "what about me?"

3) The reactor wants to be right.
4) The reactor is either trying to connect or trying to separate in order to feel safe.

<u>The four things communication and emotional intimacy demands:</u>

1) We need to witness our reactor and feel our fear.
2) We need to admit to our needs and feelings.
3) We need to honor ourselves and our partner.
4) We need to surrender our expectations and create a relationship that is balanced and offers a sense of safety to both partners.

Looking at how we relate to one another in our communication, we can start to see that it is not just communication alone that matters, but how we communicate to one another that will make us feel complete or disconnected. I asked the couple I was coaching to rate themselves on how well they meet the four demands of healthy communication and emotional intimacy on a scale of 1 to 5: 1 meaning they never do; 2, they do once in a while; 3, they have a habit of doing so; 4, they do so a lot; and 5, it is their way of being. Once they took a personal inventory and saw how they communicated, they were able to set goals for transforming their fear-based relationship into one that had emotional intimacy and healthy communication. You, too, can communicate effectively when you pay attention to the communication dynamics in your relationships.

> *Communicate more openly by bearing witness to your fear-based reactor within. This will allow you to transform yourself into a person who communicates more openly, lovingly, and effectively.*

NOT SAYING WHAT WE MEAN AND MEANING WHAT WE SAY PREVENTS US FROM COMMUNICATING EFFECTIVELY.

We often feel we are living an incomplete life because we are not saying what we mean, and meaning what we say. At the root of this behavior is a feeling of low self-worth and a question that sounds something like, "Am I worthy of having my needs met?"

If speaking your truth and asking in a direct way for your needs to be met is difficult for you, try this exercise:

1. Take out a piece of paper and, in the middle of the page, draw a circle about 4 inches in diameter. Inside the circle, write the words "When other people are anxious and busy, I start believing that I am a bother and, therefore, my needs will not be met."

2. Draw several little arms coming out of this circle. At the end of each arm, write one of your earliest memories about feeling like a bother or feeling that your needs would not be met. Did Mom make you feel that way when she was busy cooking? Was Dad so preoccupied with work and making money that he was unavailable to you? Was Mom busy with the little kids and unavailable to you? Were your friends growing up more needy than you were, making them unable to be supportive of you? Write short descriptions of all the life experiences you had that that made this belief you hold seem to be true.

3. Look at the diagram you just created. Notice what you've identified as your inner thoughts and the belief you hold

about getting your needs met.

Now it is time to transform how you see yourself and your life:

1. Take out another piece of paper and draw another circle. Inside the circle, write, "I can get my needs met when I directly ask for them to be met, and if they are not met right at that moment, they will be at the perfect time. When others do not meet my needs right away, I will say, "Hmm . . . isn't that interesting . . . I wonder what is going on with them right now that they cannot see the wonder of me?" This belief, and this question, will lead you to be curious as well as compassionate toward others.

2. Draw two arms coming out of the circle. At the end of one of the arms, write "I am value" and at the end of the other arm write "I am love."

3. Focus often on this new way of abundant thinking and believing. Remember it when you want to ask for your needs to be met. Stay open, curious, and trusting, and allow your needs to be met.

Direct communication and affirming our self-worth helps us create the life we want and sustain it. It also makes us feel complete because we are accessing the wisdom, love, and power within, making us feel abundant instead of fearful, depressed, or anxious.

Becoming aware of the specific words you use will help you in becoming a more effective and direct communicator. For example, if you want someone to call you, do you say, "It would be nice to hear from you," "Call me if you get a chance," or "I would really like to hear from you some time today"? Notice that each successive statement makes the request clearer. In the last statement, the desired outcome is very clear, giving the listener the exact formula to meet your needs.

Often, people will complain about being hurt and disappointed that their needs have gone unmet, when in fact, it is because they were not specific enough when communicating their needs to others. Underneath this more passive, indirect communication lies a belief that we are not worthy and therefore, our needs will not be met.

We are powerful human beings-powerful beyond our imagination-and will create that which we are thinking about, although what we are creating may not take the exact form we're expecting, or come about exactly when we expect it to. If you are thinking that you will not get your needs met, you will be passive and unclear in your requests and will ultimately create a self-fulfilling prophecy. You won't get what you want and will say, "I knew it!" If you believe you are worthy and will get your needs met, and you are open to how and when those needs will be met, you will communicate your needs in a clear and direct way and they will be met.

Sometimes, even when you are open and clearly communicating, you must wait for things to line up before you get exactly what you want. This can be true as you are waiting for the perfect house to be available to buy, the right relationship to appear, or just the right job to be offered to you. The universe is asking you to be patient while everything gets lined up for you.

When you say what you mean, and mean what you say, you will realize how effective communication helps you to create the life you want.

Practice clear and direct communication with yourself and others. Say what you mean, and mean what you say. This will ensure that you get your needs met in one form or another, in perfect timing.

EIGHTH PIECE:

GET CREATIVE!
DISCOVER THE FIELD OF POSSIBILITIES

Getting creative, the eighth and final piece of the personal leadership puzzle, means letting go of limited thinking, imagining what we want, expressing our desires directly, and being open to whatever possibilities may come to us so that we can obtain what we want in perfect timing. It requires that we let go of our attachments to how and when our wishes will be fulfilled, step into the unknown, and trust that the universe will provide.

To get creative, we must look at our tendency to think in certain patterns of limited thinking which prevent us from getting into a creative state in which we are open to possibilities. Limited thinking comes in many forms:

- **Either/or Thinking:** believing we have to choose from two, and only two, options.

- **Black-and-white Thinking:** believing that there is only one right way.

- **Deprivation Thinking:** believing that you are not "enough," someone else isn't "enough," or there just aren't enough options available.

The habitual pattern of engaging in limited thinking keeps us from having a complete life because we limit our thoughts to yes or no, good or bad, right or wrong, can or cannot, will or will not, and so on. When we get creative, we simply ask, "How might I (blank)?" Asking the question "How might I (blank)?" is the first step in getting creative. Being open and waiting with positive expectancy is the second step in getting creative.

Creativity allows us to be open to what is best for the all, and to partner with our Divine Creator, our world, and others to co-create what we desire. It allows us to be open to receiving solutions that we could not have thought of on our own, because on our own, we find it very hard to be completely open to the idea that it is possible to meet the core needs of all the people involved. When we get creative, we don't have to compromise, which would cause each party to get only some of their needs and desires met, leaving them feeling incomplete. When we choose what is best for the all, everyone in the situation gets his or her needs met, including us. The solution comes in some "A-ha!" moment when we receive the idea unexpectedly. We recognize that we did not conjure it up, and that it was a gift from our creativity.

To get creative and discover the field of possibilities before you, you have to let go of your preconceived notions and limited thinking and begin with a blank canvas. You have to let go of any script that tells you how you "should" act or feel in a particular situation. You have to give up the "judger" inside you, who engages in black-and-white thinking and believes that there is only one right way. Letting go of your preconceived notions and your judger allows you to be open to options that limited thinking blinds you to. This isn't to say you give up your moral code or values. It means that you stay open, trusting, and allowing yourself to recognize that perhaps something bigger is going on than what meets the eye right in this moment. By staying open to Spirit, you stay rooted in love and don't get into fear-based thinking that blinds you to the options that may be there for the good of the all. From this open perspective, you can get creative by allowing answers to come to you and therefore experiencing the "A-ha!" moments that come when you know that your creative Spirit just presented you with a miracle.

LIFE IS LIKE A RIVER. WE MUST TRUST IN ITS TIMING AND ALLOW IT TO FLOW INSTEAD OF LIVING IN ACCORDANCE WITH OUR FEAR, JUDGMENT, AND DESIRE TO CONTROL MATTERS.

Being creative isn't just coming up with clever ideas, which is what many of us think it is limited to. Creativity also includes opening yourself up to the unknown and the opportunities that will present themselves to you without you having to work at creating them. By staying in this creative and open state, and letting go of the fear that pulls you out of it, you will find that new ideas and opportunities will come to you easily.

One day, when I went to pick up some supplies I needed at one of my vendors' shops, I was reminded of this truth. I was surprised to see that the gentleman who usually waits on me from behind the counter was limping as he approached me. Noticing this, I asked, "Did you hurt yourself recently?"

To my surprise, he said, "No, I hurt myself in a car accident years ago."

When I asked this question, I never expected that response, yet somehow I knew he had a need to share and that perhaps there was even more to the story. I felt an inner conflict knowing this, because while I wanted to hear his story, I had promised my daughter I would meet her at our health club a few minutes after I dropped off my materials. Noticing my inner conflict, I asked my Creator within, "What is it that I really want to create in my life?" The answer came to me quickly: "spiritual transformation." I've always said that my mission is to help myself and others to transform spiritually, and yet as I faced this unexpected opportunity, I was struggling to be open to it. I could hear my fear-based thought that I wasn't going to have enough time to work out. In my fear, I quickly judged my daughter, who I imagined would be upset because I left her alone at the health club, not knowing what was going on. This made me want to control the conversation with this man so that I could alleviate my fear. Realizing that I could transform my fear-based thoughts and be more spiritual in this moment, I chose to stay and be fully present for the man and his story.

He picked up on my openness to hear more and said, "A drunk driver hit me and killed my son. I survived, but got this bum knee."

When I had asked about his knee, I hadn't expected his response to be such a tragic one. Once again, I could feel my limited thinking and fear-based thoughts visiting me, making me believe for a moment that this man was a victim of circumstances, judging his story to be a tragic one. Noticing this, I remained fully present and listened as he continued with his story, waiting to hear the miracle in all of it.

"Life has been one difficulty after another. . . ." he said, respectfully pausing to make sure that I was willing to listen to him.

I had always felt that this gentleman was in touch with his spirituality. It wasn't anything in particular that he said or did that gave me this impression. He just seemed to be full of light and love, and his words and actions always seemed heartfelt to me.

I felt that now was the time to share with him my perceptions about him, so I said, "That's interesting. I knew nothing about you and your story until today, but something about you resonated in me, and you always seemed to me to be a very spiritual person. It makes sense to me now that I know you have been through difficult times. I think people who have experienced difficulty have a depth to them-or they have a real chip on their shoulder."

He admitted that coming to a place of faith was neither easy nor permanent for him.

"Faith, to me, is like a river. It ebbs and flows," he told me. "Four months after my son was killed, my mother died of cancer, then my father quickly remarried and, two months later, he was found hanging in his garage. I have experienced violent death, terminal illness, and suicide. People of faith tell me that God never gives us more than we can handle, but all of that is more than I would like to handle, thank you."

Knowing that he was paraphrasing a Bible verse that someone had probably quoted to him to try to make him feel better, I responded, "I know. I'm like you-I don't like it when people quickly throw Bible verses at me just to soothe me. It feels so unsympathetic, doesn't it?"

"Yeah. I have a degree in psychology and that doesn't help much either when you're in the thick of your own pain."

I knew that the best way to support him was to just listen, letting the conversation flow where he needed it to go, without allowing my fear and judgment to control it so that I could soothe my own self by making him feel better. I tried to feel the pain along with him so that my empathy could connect our hearts to truth and love, leading us both to awaken to whatever we each needed to understand.

As I focused on remaining empathetic and listening to him, he spoke his truth, "Yeah, I know God gave me a sense of humor and resilience to equip me for all of this, but I would've preferred another gift. I often tell Him, 'My name is John, not Job!'"

I laughed, knowing he was referring to Job in the Bible, the man God tested by taking away from him everything that he loved. Job, too, wrestled with his faith, but ultimately, found a deeper connection with God, just like this man had admitted was happening to him. By the end of the conversation, I could see that although he sometimes was afraid of what shoe might fall off next, and may at times judge God for not "protecting" him, I could see that he ended up having faith that things happen for a reason, even if he couldn't quite understand why they unfolded the way they did.

On my drive to the club to meet my daughter, I reflected on my conversation with the man and thought more about how God works in mysterious ways. I also thought about how my need to be in control of my life often robs me of the joy of life's little surprises-the small moments that help me create that which I claim I want to create. Thinking about this, I realized that it isn't the circumstances we are in that cause us to feel pain, it is our need to have the circumstances match our expectations. When we realize that life is like a river and we must let it flow, we can experience the wonder of creation.

At that moment, I decided to not worry about the time, or what else might happen unexpectedly. I decided to just let life flow, be more open, and trust and allow that life was assisting me in creating my mission.

Don't let worry rob you of the joy of noticing the opportunities that present themselves to you. Instead, use the unexpected surprises to help you create what you say you want for yourself.

WE ARE SO BUSY BEING PRODUCTIVE THAT WE HAVE FORGOTTEN THE LOST ART OF CREATING.

Our limited ideas about how to be creative can often cause us to think that if we keep ourselves busy, we can solve all of our problems and achieve all of our goals. We believe that the harder we work, the more opportunities we can create for ourselves. Sometimes it is better to work smarter, not harder. Working smarter means being aware of when our busy-ness is causing us to miss the opportunities before us, because we are moving so fast that we do not take the time to openly explore them. In our haste, we jump to quick judgments, and move on our way, sticking to our preplanned agenda.

A man I worked with, who was the president of a company, complained to me one day that one of his vice presidents was not making enough sales because he was not busy enough. He told me, "I approached him and let him know that I'm frustrated that he's taking off on Friday afternoons, and that I think he could be doing more to help us reach our goals, but he doesn't seem to consider what I have to say. Whenever I talk to him, he just shuts down or gives me excuses. I feel hopeless about reaching him and getting him to work harder and to put in more hours. A lot of times, I wonder if it would be just easier to let him go."

Sometimes, we can be so focused on what we don't want to create in our lives that we can forget the art of creating that which we want. As soon as what we don't want shows up, we either flee, saying to ourselves, "Enough already. I'm done with this!" or we fight, desperately trying to get someone else to conform to our way of thinking and behaving.

The art of creating includes five steps that are similar to the steps you would take when doing intuitive coaching:

<u>Intuitive Coaching Steps:</u>

1. Share your observations.
2. Share your feelings about what you are seeing, feeling, and experiencing.
3. Become curious about the other person's perspective and needs.
4. Share your need and vision.
5. Collaborate and create by asking, "How might we create something workable for both of us?"

When we are ready to include the eighth piece of the personal leadership puzzle and get creative, we focus on creating something new for ourselves and for the other people we are in relationship with. We stop trying to force ourselves or others into playing rigid roles or acting according to scripts, and we give up our list of "shoulds." We stop asking "What about me?"

If the president I mentioned earlier decided to get creative, he might say the following to his vice president:

1. "It seems that you are taking off a lot of Fridays lately." (sharing his observations)
2. "I'm especially concerned about this because we're not meeting our goals." (sharing his feelings)
3. "Are you concerned about meeting our goals, and if so, how do you plan on doing that if you are working fewer hours?" (being curious about the other person's perspective and needs)
4. "To feel comfortable, I need to have you draw up a plan of action for increasing your sales and share it with me so that we can collaborate on the best options." (sharing his needs and vision)

5. "How might we create something workable for both of us?" and "Is that plan workable for you, or do you have another idea that would work for the both of us and help you to meet your goals?" (collaborating and creating)

If the president were to approach his vice president in this way, he would be curious, clear, calm, and confident as he articulately communicated his needs. At the same time, he would be open to hearing what the vice president had to say and willing to collaborate with him in order to come up with a viable solution together. This is in contrast to him ignoring what is going on (fleeing) or finally getting so frustrated with the situation that he fights to make things happen his way and tries to control the other person (or, as they say in business, "micromanage" him).

It all sounds so easy on paper. So why don't we operate this way in real life? To get creative, we need to have the other pieces to the personal leadership puzzle:

1. We need to get curious about what is going on.
2. We need to get clear about what we see, feel, and need.
3. We need to get calm so that we can approach the person or situation with a feeling of empowerment instead of fear.
4. We need to find our confidence to do or say what we need to in order to begin taking action.
5. We need to get caring and be empathetic to the other person so that we are open and focused on the good of the all, not taking the other person's behavior personally.

6. We need to truly commit ourselves to the ultimate goal we have in mind.
7. We need to communicate what we observe, feel, and need.
8. We need to be open enough to create something new without being attached to the form that it takes.

Whew! That's a lot of steps to go through to get creative! No wonder we want to take the easy route and just do it or forget it! However, if you have tried those other routes as often as I have, you probably have come to realize, as I have, that skipping the eight missing pieces of the personal leadership puzzle leaves you feeling incomplete.

There is something about getting creative that makes us feel in communion with ourselves, one another, and our Creator.

Discover the lost art of creating by letting creativity lead you to new ways of being and doing things.

WHEN WE ARE OBSESSED WITH SEARCHING FOR "MORE," WE OFTEN CHOOSE TO CHARGE AHEAD WITHOUT NOTICING THE WORLD WITHIN US, AROUND US, AND BEFORE US. THIS BEHAVIOR KEEPS US FROM CO-CREATING WITH OTHERS AND FROM FEELING COMPLETE.

People who charge ahead without much regard to the world within them, around them, or before them are often referred to as insensitive. I tend to look at it differently: They just haven't learned the Butterfly Technique yet. Instead of gracefully moving through life, co-creating with others, they force themselves through life like a bull.

The Butterfly Technique is a way of being that allows us to open our wings (our blinders), look around at our world and the people in it, and then put our wings back together again (close up our blinders), so we can move about gracefully and consciously as we create the lives we want. We feel more complete when we are able to be creative because our wings are open and we are noticing all that is around us as well as receiving support and input as we move ahead. Opening our blinders from time to time keeps us from being surprised or blindsided, and having to deal with crises that get out of hand when we are not paying attention. Choosing to use the Butterfly Technique at work and at home helps us to take notice of what is happening around us so that we can creatively and strategically choose what needs to be said or done in a given situation. Using the Butterfly Technique allows us to be creative, figure out clever solutions, and be receptive to the clever solutions that appear to us without our having to wrack our brains to figure out what they might be. Once we have received the information or idea we need, we can close our blinders and move into action mode, focusing on that which we need to accomplish. The Butterfly technique helps us to be balanced: Open to our creativity and focused so that we can put our creativity into action and allow us to make it happen.

Imagine, for example, that a mother uses this technique when her children come home from school, or when she arrives at home after a long day at work. As soon as she meets her children, she opens up her blinders to notice the mood, activity, and personal demeanor of each family member. As she takes in this information, she decides what to do or say next. Does the family need to eat now, or unwind and talk first? Does everyone, including Mom, need a break before getting into the evening? This is probably in contrast to what some mothers do when they are busy preparing dinner, or exhausted from work. In these cases, they have their blinders closed and hardly notice what is happening around them because they are busy and focused on what they need to accomplish in the moment and what they need to do next. Instead of quickly moving from one task to another, such as defrosting the meat, making the salad, cooking the food, and so on, they could use the Butterfly Technique to pause for a moment in between tasks, open their blinders, and take note of what is happening around them as they make dinner. Using the Butterfly Technique keeps us from being blindsided later, because we didn't notice any sign of an undesirable behavior or situation that was starting to unfold.

As women, we often struggle with the dilemma "Do I stay home with my children or not?" I believe we are asking the wrong question. I believe the question ought to be, "How might I be more present for my children?" It doesn't matter whether a mother is working outside of the home or not; what matters is how present she is when she is present. Being a full-time, stay-at-home mom but not enjoying it, or continually being preoccupied with other activities, can actually do more damage than good to our children. It sends out a message that says "You and your needs are not important" and "You are not worth my attention."

On the other hand, if we practice using the Butterfly Technique and ebb and flow between connecting with our children and doing our work while still being present, we send out a message that says, "You are important, but you are not the center of the universe. We all must cooperate and co-create together." If there is a conflict between our child's need for our undivided attention and our need to attend to a task, we can ask the child, "How might we find a time to talk that works for both of us?" If we do this, our children will be able to have high self-esteem but not an attitude of false entitlement. It's an important balance for us to strike, for ourselves and for our children if we want them to grow up to be highly functioning adults that can co-create the lives they want to live.

Being present in the moment and going with the ebb and flow is also important at work. I have heard countless bosses say that they feel like they have to be at work all of the time in order to "babysit" their employees. Yet when I ask further questions about how they spend their time when they're at work, I find that, although they are at the office many hours each week, they are not fully present, noticing what is going on around them. The employees will often confirm this. Whether the boss's door is open or not, they will complain that he or she is often busy and seems unapproachable. Because the boss has his or her blinders shut most of the time, they are not aware of what is going on with the employees. Again, it's not how much time they are present in the office that matters, it's how much time they are present in the moment, and approachable, that matters.

Other business management people I know and work with, on the other hand, seem to have the Butterfly Technique down pat. They fly in and out of the office, often traveling or working from a remote office, and still seem to have a finger on the pulse of their company: They always know what is happening back at the main office. How do they do it? They have learned to slow down, get curious, get clear about what it is they want to know, and then get creative with others as they notice and address problems. By using the Butterfly Technique and maintaining their presence in the present, they are able to connect in creativity with others even when they are miles away.

Try the Butterfly Technique. Close your blinders when you must in order to get your tasks done, but then open them up and notice what is happening around you. Being open and creative requires you to be present in the moment.

CREATIVITY ALLOWS US TO GET READY, TO AIM, AND THEN TO FIRE INSTEAD OF FIRING, HOPING EVERYONE IS READY, AND THEN WONDERING, "WHAT'S OUR AIM?"

To get creative means we pause to *get ready* to create something new, make sure we *aim* in the direction we want to go, and then *fire* with all of our heart and soul to create that which we desire. Creating in this order, instead of firing before getting ready and aiming, will save us a lot of time and energy in the long run.

Imagine for a moment that thoughts create feelings and that our feelings are energy, like gas in the gas tank of a car. Being aware of our energy is important if we want to create something new. Think about it: If you put bad fuel in your gas tank too often, you will eventually experience engine problems. Fueling up your "creative tank" with positive thoughts and focus will help you to get to your destination.

Also, imagine that our feelings about something will determine our behavior choices, and those behavior choices will create the results we see in our life. To enter the field of new possibilities and begin to create, we need open-mindedness and energy-that is, the right thoughts and the positive feelings they create. We need to be curious, clear, calm, and confident so that we can *get ready* and openly observe what is happening around us and inside of us. As we gather this data, we can consider input from others, our world, and from our inner knowing so that we can *aim* in the direction that we are being guided to go. This process requires that we gather the following pieces of the personal leadership puzzle: caring, commitment, communication, and creativity. Then, to sustain the life we want, we need to be able to access the pieces of the personal leadership puzzle and use them to continue to feel passionate about what we are creating and to behave in ways that allow us to create what we say we want for ourselves *(firing)*.

When we are creative, we slow down and are able to get ready, to aim, and to fire. Moving too quickly to solve a problem can take you in a direction you don't want to go in if you haven't taken the time to reflect or get others' input.

When I think of the process of *ready-aim-fire* as a creative process, I think of a client who just acquired a large account and was quick to decide to expand their facilities as a result. When I asked him, "How are you feeling about this new client?", he said, "Excited and scared." When I probed further, it became apparent that he was feeling "not enough." He had been in a situation like this before and it had blown up in his face because he had put all of his eggs into one basket, overinvesting in the hope that this one client would cause his business to take off. He had also had employee issues at the time, but didn't deal with them because he was so busy working out the kinks in his relationship with the new client. In that experience, he created emotional muck, believing that he was not "enough" to deal with his employees and his new client. Many of those employees left, while the others took advantage of his vulnerability and asked for raises. Feeling stuck in the emotional muck of his own limited thinking, he gave them more money, without holding them accountable to any standard of performance.

Now, with this new expansion opportunity, he had a chance to do it differently. His first inclination, just like before, was to speed things up and impulsively solve his current financial problems by meeting the client's expansion requests. But because he had found the eighth piece to the personal leadership puzzle, get creative, he was able to slow things down and get creative first, ensuring that everyone was ready, that they had a mutually beneficial aim, and they were all in sync so that he could fire, carrying out his plan of action.

Becoming creative would allow him to ask these three questions:

- How might I get ***ready***? Who, besides me, needs to get ***ready***?
- What is my ***aim***? What do others think the ***aim*** ought to be?
- Who needs to be in sync so that we can ***fire*** ahead?

In the past, his approach was more like "Fire! Are we ready? Oh no . . . what's our aim?"

Being caught up thinking we need to do more, more, more instead of letting ourselves experience our creativity can cause us to wonder later on, "Why am I not fulfilled and effective?" I see people in organizations expanding aimlessly, people in their personal lives acquiring things and relationships without thought, often in an unconscious response to wanting more, and still feeling incomplete once they have arrived at their goal. If only they would slow down to get creative, they would find that creativity takes less time and energy than just doing more and more, and it will get us where we need and want to go.

Slow down to get creative, because in the long run, it will save you time.

EITHER/OR THINKING AND DEPRIVATION THINKING ARE THE TEMPTATIONS WE FACE WHEN WE ARE CONSIDERING ABANDONING OUR CREATIVE SELF.

As we acquire the eighth piece to the personal leadership puzzle, we begin to recognize we must give up either/or thinking and deprivation thinking and instead ask, "How might I?"

Either/or thinking, which derives from deprivation thinking, is rooted in the belief that what we are asking for is too much and that there are not enough options out there for us. It causes us to see a limited field of possibilities. You hear this kind of limited thinking all the time, when people make statements such as:

- There are no good men out there. They are all married or in relationships.
- The kind of guy you want doesn't exist.
- You can't have a thriving relationship and a great career.
- If you have a great career and a thriving relationship, you certainly can't be in good physical shape. You won't have time to work out or eat right.
- You either work for humanity and are poor, or you get rich by taking advantage of others.
- You can't have your cake and eat it, too.

I briefly faced my old pattern of limited thinking this last summer when I began to date a man who was not very emotionally or physically available, except on his terms. For a short period of time, I bought into his rationalizations that he didn't have enough time to give me what I wanted, that he was not emotionally available enough because he was recovering from an old relationship, and that he just wasn't good enough at "all this relationship stuff."

It didn't take long before I realized that I was believing that I either had to be the understanding woman or turn into the nasty, demanding woman that we all have a favorite nickname for (it starts with a *B*, just in case you aren't feeling intuitive today). I also noticed within myself a tendency to focus on his good qualities and rationalize his weaknesses away because my deprivation thinking was at play, reminding me that, "There just aren't any better men out there."

Realizing that I was buying into limited thinking, I shifted away from my old thought patterns and chose to directly communicate with him, inviting him to create something different from what each of us had in the past. In his former relationships, the women had complained of his unavailability and then left the relationship because they were not getting their needs met. I knew that he had a difficult time seeing his part in the co-creation of a relationship that wasn't working because he was feeling abandoned and a bit like a victim of circumstance. I, too, had been in relationships that were like this, but I was coming from the opposite side of the fence: I was the woman who felt she could never get her needs met in a relationship and finally left when I had enough of taking crumbs. This time, I was going to handle matters differently, for the good and growth of the all. I was going to speak up early on and see if we could co-create a relationship that would be mutually satisfying.

Using the effective communication process I discussed earlier to call the bird out of the bush, I began to prepare my thoughts by using the process below:

1. ***Share your observations:*** "It seems to me that your

words don't match your actions. You say you adore me and hope I do not give up on the relationship, yet..."

2. *Share your feelings and experience:* "I'm feeling confused and unvalued since you only seem to be available on your terms. But when I want and need you, you often rationalize away my needs by saying you are busy instead of working with me to find a solution that works for both of us."

3. *Be curious about their perspective and needs:* "I'm wondering...what is that about for you and what is your vision for a relationship?"

4. *Share your need:* "For me, I desire a relationship where two people mutually consider each other's needs and desires by communicating and collaborating on creative solutions that work for both. Is that something you want in a relationship too, or are you looking for a woman who will be there when you need her, but who won't ask you to deal with her needs and wants when it's inconvenient for you to do so?"

5. *Collaborate and Create:* "How might we create something workable for both of us then so that you and I both can keep the other things in our life that are important to us, yet work on the relationship and meet each other's needs?"

I knew that practicing *ready-aim-fire* was important in my dating life as well as in my consulting work, as it would help me to have an authentic conversation with him and be open minded about whether I could have this type of relationship with him or if I needed to find someone else who was more *ready* for this type of mutual relationship. Asking the questions above would help me to know whether we were *aiming* in the same direction. If so, we could both be on *fire*, experiencing the kind of relationship we both dreamed of. If not, I was going to be open and creative, and trust that this would work out or something better was in store for me.

Working through my old pattern of either/or thinking and deprivation thinking helped me to realize that I could create the kind of relationship I wanted. In the past, when it looked like I would not get my needs met in a relationship, I grew weary and anxious, believing that all male-female relationships were hard work. Now, looking back, it wasn't the relationships that were hard work and causing me to be weary, it was my tendency to rationalize away my partner's behavior and abandon myself that caused my depression and anxiety.

Using the eight pieces of the personal leadership puzzle, I am now able to notice a situation in a relationship and have curiosity and clarity, as well as a sense of calm and confidence, a caring heart, and a commitment to myself and the good of the all. I'm able to stay open to communicating with the other person and hold on to my intention of creating something mutually satisfying. I can do this because I let go of preconceived notions about the outcome. Having this new, abundant thought process keeps me feeling complete in my life, even when I don't know what the outcome will be, because I am not abandoning myself.

Knowing that no matter what relationship I am in, at work or at home, I will have to practice using the eight pieces of the personal leadership puzzle, I can let go of my attachment to the outcome and be creative.

Creativity allows us to form effective and mutual partnerships that are based on the art of honoring ourselves and others by focusing on the highest good of the all. When we do this, we act toward each other in a way that honors all involved, and at the same time, we honor the Creator within us. This allows us to feel complete.

Stay open to how your needs will be met and "get creating." This will help you to live a complete life because you will stop abandoning your creative self.

THE WAY IN WHICH OUR LIFE UNFOLDS IS SOMETIMES UNEXPLAINABLE. BUT THE CHOICE TO BE COMPLETE, IN ANY SITUATION, IS ALWAYS OURS, AND IS ATTAINABLE IF WE MAKE THE CHOICE TO STAY CONNECTED WITH OUR CREATOR.

Stepping into the unknown and allowing life and relationships to simply unfold rather than trying to micromanage them can be very scary for most of us. In fact, the Holmes-Rahe Stress Test states that all of the major stressors are associated with a life change, whether that change is considered good or bad, so that getting married can be as stressful as getting divorced. The fact that we experience the same amount of stress whether a change is positive or negative proves that we prefer predictability over spontaneity. This is why we tend to hold onto old habits, patterns of thinking and being, preconceived roles, jobs, and relationships even when we are not happy. We stay where we are rather than enter into the unknown. When we think about what might happen if we were to change, we think about the worst possible scenarios and let our worries about what might happen keep us from making changes.

I have known many people who thought their situation would never change but it did: Marriages that seemed happy were suddenly over; jobs that seemed secure were downsized. Sometimes, these unexpected changes were very positive: chronic financial problems were solved by the money generated by one great idea; people who had gone bankrupt went on to create highly successful businesses; countless unsuccessful attempts to create a new product were forgotten about after one great invention; a person who could never find love finally found the partner of his dreams. Dramatic turnarounds are possible, and when we get creative, we open ourselves up to possibilities we hadn't thought about, opportunities that can lead us to create what we would like to create.

To get creating means that we hold on to the vision of what we want but let go of our attachment to the form-that is, we let go of our desire to dictate how, exactly, that vision will play out. It means stepping into the unknown and believing in the unexplainable miracle that occurs when we are ***open*** to our Creator, ***trusting*** our Creator to co-create with us what we desire, and ***allowing*** the plan to unfold in perfect timing. When we make the choice to live in a state of ***openness, trusting and allowing***, which is the process of creativity, we feel complete in any situation because we are living with an open heart, connected to ourselves and our Creator.

Living with an open heart allows us to be connected to our Creator and is an act of faith. Faith develops in us in stages:

- **Level 1: We begin to believe that there is something bigger than us that is in charge of the universe.** We may go to church to worship this force, or read about it, or practice some ritual associated with a Higher Power.

- **Level 2: We get caught up in devotion to Christ or some other form of Higher Being**, forgetting that divine wisdom resides in us, guiding us in bringing about what is for the highest good of the all.

- **Level 3: We honor the all and create mutually loving partnerships by acknowledging the Divine as we know Him as well as the creative spirit within us** that partners with our God. We show up to do our part in co-creating what we desire, just as we have been called to do.

- **Level 4: We go about our life open to the Divine and the creative spirit within.** We embody divine love and express that love to others as we form partnerships in which both parties honor one another. We trust in divine wisdom and divine timing, and allow life to unfold as it needs to.

Performing a religious ritual, such as attending church, and worshipping someone or something outside of ourselves is much easier than trusting in the God we worship and the creative spirit He created in us. When we realize that we have a responsibility to honor the guidance of God within us, and honor that same God spirit in another, we feel complete because we are connected. When we bring that God spirit to our relationships and create mutual partnerships, we are able to love others as we love ourselves, which is the ultimate and highest calling for all of us.

This is in contrast to demanding mutual relationships and equal rights which we have done in the past through acts of burning our bras and creating legislature to protect our rights. Creating mutual partnerships, from our God spirit, means we open ourselves up to the Divine and the creative spirit within and express that love to others as we form partnerships. These partnerships can come in varying forms, and are based on honoring one another, trusting in divine wisdom and divine timing, and believing that we need to allow life to unfold as it needs to.

Mutual and creative partnerships can be formed:

- ***With your children at a young age*** by honoring in them their opinion and perspective on things. Teach them about their God spirit and creator within by honoring their wisdom, love and power.

- ***With your co-workers*** by honoring their intuitive knowing, even when it doesn't make logical sense.

Get curious instead of judgmental and combative.

- *With your romantic partner* by honoring who they are in their unique strengths and weaknesses, versus falling into rigid roles regarding how men and women should act in a relationship.

- *With authority figures* by honoring your inner knowing, whether you are speaking with a doctor and you know what your body wisdom is telling you, or you are speaking with a pastor and you know what the Spirit is guiding you to do. Listen to and honor your wisdom within, while considering the wisdom of another.

- *With an expert speaker or author* by taking into consideration their point of view while comparing it to your own knowledge, viewpoints, or set of values.

Creative partnerships begin with us as we make the connection between our Creator and our creative spirit within. When we have made this connection, we are able to create mutual partnerships with others because we are honoring the creative spirit within them. When we create mutual partnerships around us, at work and at home, we are better able to build and sustain a complete life.

To build and sustain a complete life, focus on the creative spirit within you and others. From this viewpoint, you will create mutually creative partnerships that will assist you in building and sustaining a complete life.

THAT WHICH WE FOCUS ON EXPANDS.

On Wednesday, September 20, 2006, at 3:00 P.M., I sent the final draft of this book to my typesetters over e-mail, through cyberspace, without knowing what I was going to put on the dedication page. I told them, "Just leave the page blank. I will figure it out in a day or two."

The next morning, after my 7:00 to 9:00 leadership meeting with a client, I received a phone call from my sister-in-law, telling me that my one and only biological brother, Gary, had just died of a heart attack in his sleep.

My first thought was, "Oh no! I don't want this to be true!" which subsequently left me feeling sad, scared, alone, shocked, and powerless to handle the truth of his death.

As time went on, I realized that I had derailed into group think about what the death and dying experience is supposed to be like for all of us. It was easy for me to enmesh with the thoughts and feelings of those around me, that this was a sad loss and that I deserved condolences, since I still carried this belief about death from my experience losing my dad when I was 18. There was something about receiving sympathy that made me feel connected with others at this vulnerable time, perhaps because I knew that their sympathy was a form of love and support.

However, because I had worked hard at my own personal leadership skills, I began to become more open to my own experience, allowing my curiosity to emerge so that I could become clear about the reason my brother had lived only a short 48 years. As I began to ponder, I became calm and began observing others' experiences in a detached way, with compassion, as I stayed attached to my Divine Source, which made it possible for me to know what was real and true in the moment for me. This connection also surpassed any connection and feeling of love that I could've received from anyone else's condolences.

This is not to say that I stayed in a perfect place of peace, and I didn't have my own emotional meltdown from time to time. But I shifted into a higher perspective and became more curious, clear, calm and confident about what had just happened much more quickly than I had been able to in the past when my dad had died. Using my personal leadership skills allowed me to create an entirely new way of looking at this particular difficult situation of my brother's death. I began to focus on this thought, which gave me clarity and a sense of calm;

"It is what it is. My brother, Gary, has died. I wonder, why did God choose to take him at such a young age? What am I supposed to learn from his death?"

In asking these questions, I altered my emotional energy field within me and moved from feeling powerless, sad, and angry to feeling curious and open to the wisdom, love, and power of the Divine who could console me in the deepest way.

I could see that I was responding to my grief in a very different way than I did when my father died. At that time, my thoughts led me to believe that my dad's death was not fair, and that God had somehow betrayed me and that my father had abandoned me. This left me feeling angry at God and abandoned by my dad. Because thoughts create feelings that create behavior choices, this experience left me feeling disconnected from my heart and Spirit for many years, and unable to create the life I really wanted to create until I was willing to do the work that took me back to my truth.

Although "Dad" was not Gary's and my birth father, it was interesting to note that both of them died of a heart attack and that my Dad's death occurred at age 47 on September 19, while by brother's death was at age 48 on September 21. Even more interesting to me was to think about how although they were not biological father and son, they were connected in the most powerful way: through thoughts, feelings, and behavior choices. Both my Dad and brother didn't know how to love themselves well and take care of their own heart. Neither of them were willing to do the deeper work of looking at their emotional pain, so that they could work through it. Instead, both projected a very strong macho image, yet had a lot of emotional muck stirring around inside of them, which I believe eventually affected their heart. Both numbed their feelings with alcohol and nicotine.

Being committed to doing my own emotional work, I noticed when I was stuck in my own emotional muck during my time of grief over my brother's death. Instead of denying those uncomfortable feelings of sadness, powerlessness, guilt, anger, and so on, or saying to myself, "Gee, I wish that I felt differently," I recognized what I was feeling and then went deeper into the understanding of what that was all about for me. This allowed me to heal any residual beliefs about death that were still lingering, such as that death is an abandonment or betrayal. I was able to transform those thoughts and once again regain my grounding, recognizing what was real and true: My brother was going on to a better, everlasting life.

Each time that I worked through my emotional muck, I was able to become curious once again and open myself up to discovering new revelations about what my brother's life and death represented to others and myself.

Although I was committed to this personal leadership process, the most difficult time for me was the morning of the wake. Intuitively, I knew that there would be a large crowd and I was telling myself that I would feel overwhelmed and drained by it all. After all, my brother was nicknamed "Mr. Fun" by his niece, my daughter, because when we would go to the State

Fair with him, we could pass by no more than five people before we ran into someone who knew him. I remembered feeling overwhelmed just being around him and all his friends and acquaintances. Because he was so outgoing, I often felt shy by comparison. With his 6'4" athletic build, his swarthy good looks, and his ready sense of humor, Gary was always noticed and admired by all. Remembering these experiences, going all the way back to high school and remembering that my identity was "Gary Morrison's sister," caused me to feel powerless and fearful, as I recalled how small I felt at the time next to him.

Allowing myself to be open to this experience once again gave me a gateway to transform my limited thinking and to step into a new way of being. As the night of the wake approached, I began to transform my feelings of fear and inadequacy and reconnect with my power by refocusing on my curiosity about his life and death. This helped me to be open as I greeted the nearly 500 people who waited in line for 40 minutes to pay their last respects. Staying in the curious wonder of my brother's life and death, I was in awe as I heard many marvel at how he knew how to live his life with his heart open, having fun, and making every person he was with feel special. For years, I had worried about his tendency to drink and frankly, had even judged his lifestyle quite a bit at times, but after that night, I had noticed how God uses everyone to reach whoever he needs them to reach, in whatever way they need to be reached. As I met people who were on his football teams, bowling teams, basketball teams--and yes, even the bartender who served them after games--I was amazed at Gary's ability to touch their lives and open their hearts to love.

Gary lived large and showed others how to do that as well, and because he focused on that goal, he achieved it. I wanted to understand what his life was about, and because I focused on that thought that night, I heard many people answer my question. Although I will still have times of sadness and will miss my brother, I peacefully accept my brother's life and death and realize that God used it all and so did Gary. The power of the heart to attract that which we want to create continues to amaze me. It is the access point in which we meet our divine self and our Divine Creator who hears what we are focusing on and want to create.

To create the lives we want, we need to carefully observe our thoughts and feelings so that we can focus on that which we want to create, because that which we focus on will expand. Unfortunately, for years, Gary told many of us that he was afraid that he was going to die at a young age. I thought that perhaps his learning in his mid-thirties that my dad was not his biological father, so he could not have inherited Dad's lack of longevity, would help him to change his thoughts, but it didn't. I can't help wondering if Gary's worrying about dying for years didn't take its toll on his heart. I guess this is a lesson for all of us on how we are powerful creators and need to remember that what we think about we bring about.

Today, practice being conscious about your thoughts.
Are your thoughts focused on what you want to create,
or they focused on your fears? Notice where you are,
meet yourself with love, and then transform your thoughts,
so you can transform your feelings and your world.

THE PERSONAL LEADERSHIP ASSESSMENT

Choose whichever statement best describes the way you respond to situations: statement A, B, or C.

1) When a person is making a choice to do something you do not agree with, do you:
   A. Think about how that wasn't a good choice, but don't say anything
   B. Tell him that you don't understand why he made that choice
   C. Get curious, and ask, "What made you decide to do that?"

2) When you are unsure about a decision you need to make by the end of the day, do you:
   A. Fret about it all day long
   B. Ask many people what they would do
   C. Find some quiet time to reflect on what it is you want

3) When you have just found out alarming news, do you:
   A. Panic and jump in to see what you might do
   B. Gather more information right away
   C. Notice that you are feeling afraid and quiet yourself down before doing anything

4) When you are asked to do something that you are afraid you are not good at, do you:
   A. Automatically say "no" to the invitation
   B. Consider whether you might be able to participate in some way
   C. Notice that your fear is keeping you from expanding

yourself and then think about viable options

5) When you go to a restaurant and the waitress is rude to you, do you:
   A. Get rude to her
   B. Leave her a smaller tip
   C. Show kindness and ask her how her day is going

6) When you are faced with difficulty at work or at home, do you:
   A. Tend to want to tell everyone about it or just withdraw from the situation
   B. Stay busy so that you don't have to think about it
   C. Spend time reflecting on what is happening, how you feel about it, and how you could best deal with it

7) When a co-worker isn't open to your ideas, do you:
   A. Get upset
   B. Let her know that you do not feel she is open to you or your ideas
   C. Invite her to consider other viable options that could work for the both of you

8) When you and your friends cannot agree on an activity for the day, do you:
   A. Just go along with their idea so you don't ruffle any feathers
   B. Engage in whatever portion of the activity works for you
   C. Ask them how you might consider other options that would work for everyone

9) When life isn't going just as you thought it would, do you:
   A. Give up

B. Try to talk yourself out of feeling anxious or depressed
C. Realize that you are feeling anxious and depressed and go deeper into realizing what lie you are telling yourself about yourself in this situation

10) When you are feeling anxious or discouraged, do you:
A. Find something to soothe yourself, such as a drink or a cigarette
B. Tell others about how you are feeling
C. Spend time working through the emotions you are feeling so that you can get to the root cause of them

Now, let's see how you did! Add up your points.
A=1 point, B=3 points, and C=5 points.

41-50 Points: You are living a life of personal leadership! You have a conscious connection with yourself and are open to the possibilities around you. You also know how to recognize obstacles, and how to get curious, clear, and calm. When you are anxious or depressed, you quickly recognize it and transform the feeling into confidence so that you can stay committed to the life you have envisioned by using your creativity, your ability to communicate, and your caring heart.

35-40 Points: You are often leading your life by personal leadership, but sometimes you tend to let anxiety and depression get the best of you. When times get tough, you can visit the "pity-pot" for a while or believe that asking for sympathy from others is a good use of your energy. Because you do understand the difference between being in your power and feeling like a victim, you don't like to waste too much time in self-pity before you pick yourself back up. To avoid this back-and-forth cycle, go deeper into discovering the root cause behind your "pity pot." Ask yourself, "What makes me feel like a victim?"

30-34 Points: You are aware at some level that the ability to live with personal leadership will make a difference in your life, because you have experienced the benefit of that way of being. However, you are in the habit of making excuses and blaming circumstances "beyond your control" for where you are in your life. In order to grow, you will need to humble yourself and be more emotionally honest about what is going on inside of you so that you can lead your life differently. When you can take an honest emotional inventory of yourself and consciously make choices in the moment that are in your best interest and for the highest good of the all, you will see how your active leadership shapes your life.

20-29 Points: You have a desire to discover the benefits of personal leadership, but you are stuck in an old belief that you are here on this earth to make others comfortable. It's not that you don't know what you want, it is that you are afraid to claim it because of your fear of disapproval, failure, and abandonment. To embrace the personal leader that you are, focus on these feelings as they come up for you. Pay closer attention to where they show up in your body and what you tell yourself about them. Tune in to yourself before making impulsive decisions to please others. Then stretch yourself by speaking up in the moment and asking, "How might we consider (blank)?"

Change takes time. As you see a positive change in yourself, recognize your courage. Focus on how you are growing instead of what you are not doing yet. Treating yourself in this loving way will help to foster your personal transformation.

I AM COMPLETE

This drawing was inspired by a photo taken from
Susan K. Wehrley's Pewaukee, Wisconsin Lake home.

For your limited edition of this original drawing,
see our website, www.ThePersonalLeadershipPuzzle.com.